Challenges to the Cross

CHALLENGES
TO THE *Cross*

Wayne Dehoney

BROADMAN PRESS • Nashville, Tennessee

© 1962 • BROADMAN PRESS
Nashville, Tennessee

All rights reserved
International copyright secured
Third Printing

422-158

Library of Congress catalog card number: 62-9196
Printed in the United States of America
3.5O6413

Contents

To

WILLIAM WARREN DEHONEY

and

RUBY NORTHUP DEHONEY

Christian parents

whose dedication to Christ and his church was ever constant

whose family devotion and love knew no restraint

whose physical and financial sacrifices for three sons knew no limit

whose faith, deep yet simple and without gloss, set a worthy example

and laid the foundations for kingdom service in the lives of

Wayne, Eugene, and Homer

this book is affectionately dedicated

Foreword

IF I had the means to do so, I would place this volume in the hands of every freedom-loving person on this earth. I would do it not because the author is my friend, but because it has a message and challenge which is greatly needed in this hour.

With clear discernment Wayne Dehoney has put his finger on the most perplexing matters facing us today as individuals or as a nation. Dealing with such topics as communism, materialism, intellectualism, alcoholism, delinquency, ecumenicalism, and the relation between church and state, he takes the pulse of our sick society and prescribes the remedy.

Every word of this volume breathes the writer's knowledge of God's Holy Book and his conviction that the Bible has something to say to our generation. In such an atmosphere he has produced a treasure house of information which is as contemporary as the problems themselves.

Wayne Dehoney has brought forth a work whose value will not be limited to any one religious denomination. It is a book with a message for everyone who would stand in the breach for God, as through us he faces the "challenges to the cross."

First Baptist Church HERSCHEL H. HOBBS
Oklahoma City, Oklahoma

Preface

NEVER has the cross faced such a formidable array of challengers. Militant, atheistic communism, marching in seven-league boots, immediately threatens not only Christianity but the very survival of theism. Yet in our hysterical fear of Russia, we ignore with blind disregard other subtle enemies of the cross equally as ruthless, as determined in purpose, and as final in consequence.

Many people are looking to militarism and nuclear preparedness as the ultimate messiah of deliverance. The cross-bearing Jesus has little relevance for them in a world bristling with atomic stockpiles.

Incipient moral rot and social decay eats away at the very heart of an affluent Western civilization. Scientism challenges the concept of a personal, creative God, scorns revelation as truth, and offers a rationalized religion that would make God the servant of Space Age man. Alcoholism is our number one medical and social problem. Juvenile delinquency is the major crime problem, and the home is the chief breeding place of crime. The organic union of all churches is proposed on the premise that a solid Christian front, without the fragmentation of denominationalism, is needed to face effectively these enemies of the cross.

Meanwhile, concerted attacks by a powerful Church organization batter at the Constitutional wall of separation between the church and state to threaten religious freedom and the cherished American heritage of a free church in a free state.

Out of these clouds of turmoil and storm has issued the cry for a "return to religion." But that "religion" is seldom defined beyond a "sincere worship of God."

This is the complexity of the crisis in contemporary Christianity. While interpreting the current issues and defining our role as a Christian in the conflicts, I realize that both issue and solution may at times seem oversimplified. Yet it is not so much my purpose to be *exhaustive* as it is to be *decisive,* to call for immediate, direct action. In this eleventh-hour struggle for survival, the call is not to "reason why" but rather to "do or die." I have tried to reflect this sense of urgency. The book sounds a trumpet call for action; it pleads that we do battle *this day* for the cross!

I pay special tribute to a warm "fellowship of the resurrection," the congregation of the First Baptist Church of Jackson, Tennessee, whose devotion and loyalty are a constant inspiration to me as pastor and whose response to a series of sermons dealing with these issues stimulated this book.

I am indebted to Miss Mildred Snow for her tireless stenographic work; to Miss Rachel Colvin, Dr. George Schweitzer, Dr. J. P. Edmunds, and Dr. James L. Sullivan for reviewing the manuscript and making valuable suggestions; to Dr. A. V. Washburn and Keener Pharr for the opportunity to present much of this material in sermonic form at Glorieta Baptist Assembly; and to Dr. H. H. Hobbs, pulpit giant, scholar, author, and denominational statesman, who, amid the pressures of his many responsibilities, took time to review the manuscript and to write the foreword.

I present this book with a prayer that your purpose and spirit will be joined with mine in a new dedication to face these challenges to the cross with decisive Christian action.

WAYNE DEHONEY

> "We are up against the unseen power that controls this dark world, and spiritual agents from the very headquarters of evil" (Eph. 6:12, Phillips).

1. The Sickle or the Cross

ON May 29, 1957, Dr. Frederick Schwarz, authority on world communism and executive director of the Christian Anti-communist Crusade, appeared before the House Committee on Un-American Activities. He was asked, "What is your appraisal of the progress of communism?"

He replied, "By every standard test, the Communists have been making terrifying progress. They are winning and we are losing!"[1] To document his statement, he told of a visit with the president of a firm using Univac. Dr. Schwarz proposed that the mechanical brain, which makes statistical predictions free of human error, be fed the following data:

Lenin established Bolshevism with 17 supporters in 1903.

He conquered Russia with 40,000 in 1917.

By 1937, there were 170 million Communists, or 8 per cent of the world population.

From this isolated revolution in an obscure backward country, world communism has spread and now engulfs one billion people, or 37 per cent of the world population.

Ask Univac, "When will communism conquer the world?"

The answer: By 1970, communism will have conquered two billion people, or 66 per cent of the world population. By 1973, their world conquest will be complete! Unless there is dramatic human counteraction or divine intervention, the free world has only a few years left, according to Univac.

The Continuing Advance of Communism

Apparently, Russian computers concur with Univac in predicting total, imminent victory as the destiny of communism. For, at a recent international gathering of Communist leaders in Moscow, Khrushchev and Mao Tse-tung boldly announced *1973 as the target date for world domination.* Their immediate program called for the completion of the conquest of Asia and her consolidation into a solid Communist bloc, the conquest of Africa, and the creation of chaos in Europe and South America.

The *New York Times* predicted that by then China will have one billion people, an economic system roughly equivalent to that of Russia's at the outbreak of World War II, and a war machine complete with nuclear and rocket weapons. Mao was quoted as saying that China could lose three hundred million people in an atomic war and still survive.[2] Correspondent Joseph Alsop reports from Hong Kong that the agrarian reform in China is in trouble and that drouth, floods, crop failure, and famine have caused millions to die.[3] But the picture is not substantially changed. China has 650 million people. They are born at a rate increasing the population by twenty-five million a year. China could lose, by famine or war, the equivalent of the entire population of the United States, and in less than eight years births would replace it.

On Khrushchev's first visit to the United States he was bold, confident, and arrogant on his nationwide telecast. Pointing his stubby finger he said, "I prophesy that your grandchildren will live under communism." Clenching his fist he defiantly snarled, "We will bury you!" This was not a threat of atomic destruction. He was saying, "We will overrun you as we have Europe and Asia. We will take you by peaceful conquest. We will conquer you economically. We will bury you scientifically. We will defeat you with our propaganda. We will bury you as a nation!"

Since these fateful words were spoken, Russia has made steady progress in fulfilling these threats. Khrushchev said,

"We will shoot the moon and the world will see it as the red flag of communism in the night sky." They made the moon shot and took pictures of the backside. Khrushchev said, "With our scientific powers we will make the rivers of the United States run backwards. We will defy natural law." Today, hurtling through space toward the planet Venus, is a Russian rocket, launched piggyback from a satellite circling the earth. Military experts say that if Russia can launch a giant satellite into orbit and control it with such precision as to fire a rocket from it at the target Venus, billions of miles away, it would be child's play to aim a piggyback rocket armed with a nuclear warhead or a death ray at a pinpoint target a hundred miles away, earthside! Today, conceivably every city in the United States is in jeopardy of a Russian atomic missile launched from such a satellite.

When the Kennedy administration came into office, scientific advisors said, "We have lost the space race. We cannot put a man in space ahead of Russia." Three months later, on April 12, 1961, Soviet air force Major Yuri Gagarin's voice crackled back from 187.5 miles in outer space fulfilling this gloomy prediction. Nate White, business and financial editor for the *Christian Science Monitor* and an authority on Russia, said, "The productive system of the USSR is formidable, its budget directed to scientific breakthrough, its research advanced and thorough, its mathematicians the world's greatest and its work in cybernetics (the science of automatic control by electronic and mechanical processes) outstanding."[4] Russia is burying us scientifically!

Economically, Russia is burying us. Another of the administration's pressing problems is the gold outflow brought about by the loss of world markets to the Communist bloc.

Propagandawise, we are losing. I recommend the book *The Ugly American* as required reading for every citizen. It will bring tears to your eyes and a sickness to your heart. Read how we are losing the propaganda war with Russia as we perpetuate the great American tradition of the cocktail party in our embassies and assert a snobbish, swaggering superiority in dealing with other nations. While we promote gin-and-bourbon diplomacy in starched shirts and low-cut gowns, Russia is sending serious-minded, dedicated technicians by the thousands to live with the natives and win their confidence.

Communist Strategy for the Conquest of America

Neither Lenin nor Marx anticipated total war to accomplish their purpose. Instead, they proposed a strategy of infiltration, of dividing loyalties, of pitting class against class, of creating economic and political chaos, of propaganda, of the big lie. Then, at the right moment, a hard corps of trained Communists would take over a country. No armies move in, no tanks roll, no military machines move, but citizen revolutionaries just take over! Using this strategy, communism has conquered a large portion of the world without world war and without the Russian army violating a single national border.

Lenin sets forth their master plan: "First, conquer eastern Europe; then, the masses of Asia; then, we will circle the United States of America, the last bastion of capitalism. We will not have to attack it. It will fall like an overripe fruit in our hands."

A hard core of Communists have been recruited and trained in our country, looking to this day. J. Edgar Hoover in his book *Masters of Deceit* says that there are 20,000 Communists committed and dedicated to the overthrow of our government. That is exactly half the number which, in Russia in 1917, seized the reins of power. Mr. Hoover says that for every dedicated communist there are ten other functionaries who are ready to assist him in every way. Thus there are 200,000 sympathizers ready to do the bidding of these 20,000 dedicated party members in America.

Who are these Communists and their functionaries? According to the House Committee on Un-American Activities, for fifteen years the Communist party has been getting key spots in our military organization, in labor unions, among professionals, among writers, among molders of public opinion.

It has been charged that there are Communists disguised in clerical robes in the pulpits of our churches. About this witch-hunt for "pinks in the pulpit," J. Edgar Hoover says the charge is absolutely groundless. Instead, he says that "the Christian ministers in our pulpits today stand as the greatest bulwark against communism that we have."[5] Ralph Lord Roy in *Communism in the Churches,* published in 1960, gives a documented answer to this charge. There are a half-million ministers in the United States, and less than two hundred can be identified as having Communist leanings. Two hundred out of a half-million! This is one of the lowest percentages of any professional or vocational group. Of these two hundred, the great majority are not pastors of churches and hold no responsible position with their denominations.[6]

This is the crisis that challenges us. Militant communism has gone farther in forty years than Christianity in two thousand years. The Red tide has rolled across the face of the earth, engulfing a billion people, winning China, neutralizing India, bidding for Africa, throwing Europe into turmoil and confusion, infiltrating the campuses of Latin America, and encircling the United States. That tide is now hammering against the foundations of our Republic.

The Appeal of Communism—Three Half-Truths

What power drives the consuming force of communism forward? Is it guided by "spiritual agents from the very headquarters of evil," as Paul suggests? The Bible prophesies that a power called the antichrist will one day appear on earth. He will be the ultimate foe of Christianity, have world dominion as an objective, and world conflict as the means of conquest. Violence, persecution, suffering, and death will accompany the march of the antichrist. There will be a great cataclysmic end to this conflict called "Armageddon." This battle will mark the end of the age, and it will be terminated by fire when the elements will melt in a great conflagration.

Scientists have commented on the striking similarity between the description of this holocaust given in 2 Peter 3:10 and the effects of a thermonuclear blast.

But perhaps the most startling characteristic of the antichrist is that it will be a counterfeit of Christianity. *And communism, basically, is a counterfeit, a perversion, and an imitation of some of the basic appeals and characteristics of Christianity.* Communism appears as a protest and revolution against injustices and inequity, promises a world brotherhood, and has the dynamics and appeal of a religion. Regardless of whether or not we admit the possibility that communism is the antichrist of the Scriptures, the student of communism must recognize that these three half-truths or false promises of communism, counterfeits of Christianity, are primary in communism's motivation and appeal.

A protest.—First, communism arises as a protest against injustices. Wherever there is discrimination, wherever there is hunger, wherever there is persecution, the Communist finds a fertile field. He says, "Follow us and we will give you social and economic justice, human rights, and your fair share of this world's goods."

We often forget that communism is not Russian in origin. It is a Western idea. It was born in the mind of Karl Marx amid an environment of Western capitalism, not feudal Russia. Marx was born in 1818 in what is, today, a part of East Germany. He attended the University of Bonn where his mind was nurtured in a radical-student atmosphere. He became editor of a radical newspaper in France. Banished from France and Germany for his political leanings, he found refuge in England where he lived for forty years. In an attic apartment the brooding radical wrote many books and pamphlets. His two most famous books are *Das Kapital,* the bible of communism, and the *Communist Manifesto,* which sets forth the creed of communism. In recent years these two books have outstripped the Bible as the world's best sellers.

While communism was born in a dingy London attic, it

needed a more fertile field in which to root. In 1903, seventeen people found it and organized the first Communist political party in Russia. Here was gross injustice and brutal inhumanity. Ninety per cent of the peasants owned no land and had no rights. Eighty per cent of the people could not read. A wealthy, decadent church linked hands with the czar and maintained a ruthless slavery. The Communist said to the peasant boy Joseph Dzhugashvili, "Come, little Joe, follow us and we will give you a new way of life." Little Joe had seen his three brothers and sisters starve to death as peasants. Though trained for the priesthood, little Joe hung up his frock and followed the communists to find a new way of life. The world knew little Joe as Joseph Stalin!

In 1887, a seventeen-year-old Russian youth Vladimir Ulyanov watched the Royal Police seize his older brother Alexander, publicly mutilate him, cut out his tongue, cut off his ears, and then hang him at the door of their peasant hovel with orders that anyone who cut the body down would be shot. The brother's stinking body swung there until it rotted down. Is it any wonder that the bitter youth never forgot his silent oath to "change things"? The world later knew him as Lenin. With Stalin and Lenin, 40,000 others were ready in 1917 to follow in a revolution to change things and remake them according to any pattern that was new.

This is the cutting edge of communism. It moves into the areas of great human need and physical want, of oppression, and of injustice and discrimination. Communism is a protest against social injustices and promises a change. That is why it has such a hold in Bolivia. While visiting there, I was told that in 1945 seven families owned 90 per cent of the land and resources of Bolivia. For generations they had exploited the millions of Indians, who lived in filth, poverty, and ignorance and were denied land, rights, and opportunity. A communist-inspired revolution is changing Bolivia today.

News journalist Coleman Harwell, of the *Nashville Tennessean,* says that while the average per capita income in the

United States is $2,027 per year, there are a billion people in this world today whose annual income is less than $60.00 per year. Communism is saying to these one billion people that the average American earns more in two years than they earn in a lifetime. Back from a world tour and study of communism, Harwell said that the communists are saying to them, "You do not need to sleep twelve to a room if you are lucky, or sleep on the streets if you are not. You do not need to live in filth like animals and die like flies. Follow us and we will change things."[7]

Albert Colegrove, Scripps-Howard staff writer on special assignment to Latin America, said that at this point we Americans have failed to grasp the real appeal of communism. We know nothing of the poverty, futility, and suffering that plagues the great masses of this earth. For example, meet Juan Ortiz in the Republic of Panama. Juan and his family of five are jammed into a single, waterless room in a Panama City slum. About nine of every one hundred workers are jobless here. Juan is one of them. His five-year-old daughter begs on the streets. His son, eight, shines shoes. The family may lose its room tomorrow. Or meet Justo Garcia and his family of six. They are squatters in a shack on an acre of hillside land. They have no legal right to the property. The rich man who owns it has not bothered to evict them, yet. So they have the food they grow, but almost no money. Justo's wife is half blind from cataracts.

To these people, the Communists offer hope and revenge on a society that has relegated them to the trash heap of humanity. "March with us! We will take the land from the rich and give it to you! We will feed your children and heal your wife!" they promise. The word "communism" is never mentioned. Reds do not waste their energies trying to explain Karl Marx to hungry men who cannot read or write. They go right to the basic yearnings of these people.

Colegrove states the issue tersely: *"You cannot fight communism with anti-communism alone. You cannot fight hope by scorning it.* You cannot defeat communism by exposing Castro or Nikita Khrushchev to people who are only faintly aware of either man—but who desperately know what they want, and who feel that any change might make things better and couldn't make things any worse [*Italics mine*]."[8]

Two spirits are loose in this world proposing to change it. There is the Spirit of Christ, who looked with compassion on the multitudes and saw them diseased, hungry, and like sheep without a shepherd. Then there is the spirit of Marx coming also to these in distress and need. Wherever there is disease, hopelessness, economic injustices, filth, poverty, children dying—these two spirits are there to compete.

Ours is a clear choice. *We* may change the future of the underprivileged masses of the world through *Christian concern* and sharing, or *communism* will change it by the power of *class revolution.* But either way, this much is certain: The impoverished masses of the world are in revolt and demand a change. While we Christians sit content and self-satisfied in our Bible classes, and comfortable in our air-conditioned churches, indifferent to the yearnings of a billion people who seek a better way of life, the communists are out there now, in every village and bypath to the furthest corners of the earth saying, "Follow us, and we will change your world!"

A brotherhood.—The second half-truth of communism is the promise of world brotherhood. Many years ago I saw a poster that was brought out of China by a journalist. It pictured a communist flag carried by four strong muscular arms —one white, another yellow, another black, and another brown. I was told that the slogan in Chinese characters read, "Arise, brothers; together we conquer the world." I was told that the poster had been taken from a British-owned recreation park in Shanghai reserved for the exclusive use of white military, diplomatic, and missionary personnel. The park was posted with signs reading "No dogs—no Chinese allowed."

This, then, is the story of a segregated park in Shanghai and a Chinese poster on brotherhood. Twenty-five years later finds the white man driven out of China and the park no longer segregated. The poster is gone, but the Communist ideal of brotherhood is marching with seven-league boots across Asia and into Africa, enlisting millions. And multi-colored arms still carry the Red flag calling, "Arise, brothers, black, yellow, brown—together we conquer the world."

Though I cannot personally verify this story, I can speak with assurance that the racial conflicts of Little Rock, the bombings of Negro homes in Birmingham, a white mob rioting and burning a freedom-rider bus in Montgomery—all of these stories made blazing headlines in Tokyo, Africa, and Latin America. You see, six out of seven people in this world are colored. The communists say, "See! The Americans are the enemies of the colored peoples of the world, your enemies, and you outnumber them six to one!"

Hard realists that they are, the Communists long ago junked the doctrine of white supremacy. They promise a world brotherhood to the nonwhites who make up six-sevenths of the world's population. Need I say more! If Christian principle does not motivate us toward brotherhood with those of other races, surely the instinct for self-preservation should!

A religion.—The third appeal of communism is that it has the dynamics of a religion. Dr. Josef Rysan of Vanderbilt University said:

The Communist Party possesses its *Holy Writ,* body of *dogmas* and *creeds,* its *cult* and *ritual,* its *prophets, messiah, saints, martyrs, missionaries, apostates, heretics, inquisitors, sacred symbols* and *shrines.* The keystone of the Marxist Church is the *revelation* of the *Great Prophet Marx.* Ironically, while reason-obsessed Christian theologians have timidly minimized the revelatory character of the Bible and subjected it to merciless scientific criticism, *Communist theologians have treated Marx's writings as the revelation and the Holy Script of Communism.* Stalin's pamphlet *Dialectic and Historical Materialism* is considered the *catechism. Any deviation* from orthodoxy is punished as an unpardoned heresy. The Marxist Church has also evolved the device of public *recanting* and *penance* which is mostly reserved for minor sinners among the Soviet scientists and artists. Marxism and organized Communism are indeed a secular religion and a political church.[9]

As a religion, communism motivates its adherents to ceaseless activity in winning the world. Dr. Sam Moffett, veteran missionary, witnessed the Communist invasion of China. He said that every soldier was a missionary. Each soldier carried his gun and the standard works of communism. He was constantly seeking converts. The Communists conquered by force and then gathered classes to teach, indoctrinate, and brainwash the people. The converts were then made missionaries and sent out. Dr. Moffett compared this missionary zeal to that of New Testament Christianity where the scattered ones went witnessing to win. One cannot help but compare this Communist zeal for winning converts with the complacent visitation program for evangelism in the average Christian church!

J. Edgar Hoover has contrasted the fervor and dedication of the Communist to that of the average Christian:[10]

First, the Communists emphasize the importance of continually returning to the original source of their beliefs to secure inspiration and power. They daily study the bible of communism. Yet how few Christians take any time daily to read our Bible? How often each day do we quench our spiritual thirst by digging deep in the wells of our faith? Pressured and troubled by tensions and anxieties, do we turn regularly to the Scriptures for strength as the Communists turn to *Das Kapital* and the *Communist Manifesto?*

Second, Communists stress not only the reading of Marx, Engels, and Lenin but also reading them constantly on a daily or weekly schedule, never neglecting the habit. They say that to be a good Communist calls for a lifelong devotion to studying Marxism-Leninism. Yet, as Christians, most of us read the Bible only on special occasions! How many of us set aside a certain amount of time each day in the week to make a consistent study of the Word of God? Do we regard the Bible as for children only? Have we outgrown it as adults? These questions strike at the very heart of our religious life.

Third, the Communists have no use for mere ceremonial avowal of Marxism, or a shallow intellectual acceptance of its ideals. Every Communist is under ceaseless pressure to deepen his insight, knowledge, and comprehension of communism. Yet, in contrast, how many Christians are church members in name only and know nothing, and care less, about the doctrinal undergirdings of their faith?

Fourth, at all times the Communists test the relationship between theory and action. They say, "We study for the sole purpose of putting into practice what we have learned." Yet here is the big gap in the Christian community, the wide gap between faith and action, between profession and practice.

Finally, the party stresses the development of the politically mature comrade, the specialist, who will be charged with the supreme missionary task of the party. These specialists are recruited, trained, supported, and sent out as missionaries in the Communist revolution to win the world. We Christians also seek to win a world. We, too, are working for a revolution—not of the sword, but of the spirit. But our cause gets only a token of our money, little of our time and interest, and only a very few talented and trained young people.

The Christian Tragedy

Why have men responded to communism as a religion? It has been a negative response of turning away from perverted Christianity that was formal, ritualistic, dead in spirit, and separated from the life and the needs of men. Stalin studied for the priesthood! Karl Marx wrote a stimulating, theologically correct essay "Union with Christ" at seventeen years of age! But a cold, spiritless, decadent church lost them.

Men are attracted to communism because deep in the heart of every man is a God-created vacuum—he *must* believe in something. He seeks a power outside himself, a cause greater than himself, to which he can give his loyalty and life. Every man instinctively seeks to give himself to something eternally significant. Communism says to the radical who has rejected organized Christianity, "Here is a religion you can sink your teeth into. Here is something worthy of your dedication and devotion. Here is action! We change the world!"

Herein is the tragedy of tragedies. Communism is filling the emptiness created by our Christian stagnation, neglect, and indifference. In 1935 in Red Square, Moscow, an American newspaperman Charles Wells was watching a parade of 40,000 communist youths. It was bitter cold. Snow flurried in the air. There was a bottleneck down the street, and the parade was marking time. They began to chant in unison deep, guttural Russian. He could not catch the words, and turned to a Russian correspondent asking, "What do they sing?" "Oh, Comrade, it is nothing. They just sing, 'We may be cold, we may be hungry, but we change the world.'" It is *nothing!* Cold, hungry, but "We march to change the world!"

Today, these young people are marching to change the world. But though they should win the world, it would not be changed. It would still be the same old world—full of greed, selfishness, sorrow, and heartbreak. Yet there is an even greater tragedy. *We have the message that will change the world— the only message.* But we are never cold, never hungry, and we care little about changing anything!

Today, two armies march! Two banners call for men's allegiance—one the sickle, the other the cross. J. Edgar Hoover set forth the choice that faces every American: The issue is "communist domination or Christian rededication."[11]

"And there went out another horse that was red: and power was given to him that sat thereon to take peace from the earth, and that they should kill one another: and there was given unto him a great sword" (Rev. 6:4).

2. Sword or Spirit?

THE United States has spent $300 billion in the last decade on weapons to stop the Red tide, and still it spreads in Asia, Africa, the Caribbean, and Latin America. Yet we continue in the blind faith that, somehow, a bigger budget for atomic weapons, a stronger military force, and superior arms will somehow stop communism and save us. But ultimate victory over communism is beyond a sword or missile. Military might can enforce law in a lawless world. But weapons alone can never defeat communism.

Back of communism are powerful dynamics that are moving millions of people. Communism, as a counterfeit of Christianity, is launched as a protest against injustices. It promises a world brotherhood, and it has the motivations of a religion. The power of this dynamic is reflected in the statement, printed in the *Presbyterian Survey,* of a young Communist:

The socialist cause . . . is my life, my business, my religion, my hobby, my sweetheart, wife, and mistress, my bread and meat. I work at it in the daytime and dream of it at night. It is my alter-ego.

Therefore, I can't carry on a friendship, a love affair, or even a conversation without relating it to this force which both drives and guides my life.

I have already been in jail because of my ideas, and if neces-

sary I am ready to go before a firing squad. A genuine radical lives
in virtual poverty. He turns back to the party every penny he
makes above what is absolutely necessary to keep him alive. We
constantly look for places where the class struggle is the sharpest,
exploiting these situations to the limit of their possibilities. We lead
strikes. We organize demonstrations. We speak on street corners.
We fight cops.

Radicals don't have the time or the money for many movies
or concerts or T-bone steaks or decent homes and new cars. We've
been described as fanatics. We are. Our lives are dominated by
one great, over-shadowing factor—the struggle for socialism. We
Communists have a philosophy of life which no amount of money
could buy. We have a cause to fight for, a definite purpose in life.
We subordinate our petty personal selves into a great movement
of humanity. We have a morale, an *esprit de corps* such as no
capitalistic army ever had; we have a code of conduct, a way of
life, a devotion to our cause that no religious order can touch.
And we are guided not by blind, fanatical faith but by logic and
reason, by a never-ending education of study and practice.

We are adequately compensated by the thought that each of
us is, in his small way, helping to contribute something new and
true, something better to mankind.

We have branded communism as a counterfeit Christianity,
or a secular religion capitalizing on the weaknesses and failures of Christianity in its great leap forward. Nevertheless, the
basic philosophy, ultimate values, methods, and final objectives of communism are the antitheses of Christianity.

The Evils of Communism

First, communism is atheistic—relentlessly, totally atheistic.
In its inception, Marx said, "It is not religion that creates man,
but man who creates religion. It is an opiate of the people."
From that beginning, and through its present leadership, communism is atheistic. Khrushchev said, "We will remain the
atheists that we have always been."[1] Never expect a softening
on this point. Do not let reports of religious toleration mislead
you.

Many religious people live in communist territory. For example, the largest national body of Baptists outside the United States is in Russia. Other denominations, also, continue to operate in the satellite countries. But communism is still atheistic, and it tolerates religion and the Christian church only as a *temporary whim of expediency.* Communism declares there is no God and is committed to the eradication of all belief in him.

A second evil in communism is what it believes about man: Man is only a material machine. Karl Marx said the Christian idea that God made man in his own image "is only a projection of man's ego." Communism believes man is only what he eats, matter, and motion. He is a social being, molded by economic forces, a product of society rather than heredity. Man has no freedom. He is like the cells in the body. One cell alone means nothing. All cells work for the good of the state. The only difference between man and animal is his rational ability. William A. Foster, former head of the Communist Party in the United States, wrote in his book *The Twilight of World Capitalism,* "Henceforth the evolution of the human species must be done artificially by the conscious action of man himself."

A third evil is that communism is immoral. If there is no God, and if man is not made in the image of God but is simply an accumulation of matter, then there is no such thing as morality. A thing is right as long as it serves communism, wrong if it does not. A communist may resign one job and accept another, move from one town to another, leave family and friends, get a divorce and remarry, lie, cheat, and steal to help the cause. All this becomes right in the light of the end served. Thus force, violence, brutality, mass murder, and wholesale purging become morally acceptable methods of operation for communism. Winston Churchill asked Joseph Stalin, "How many peasants did you liquidate in the last reform?" He smiled and held up his stubby fingers, "Oh, maybe ten million in four years. It was bad but it had to be done."

A fourth evil is that communism claims *no absolute stand-ard of truth.* The communist will shrewdly lie to any group to accomplish his objectives. Communism studies to determine the basic self-interest of a group and then fashions a program to appeal to that group. As George Sisler, promotion editor of the Memphis *Commercial Appeal,* said in an address:

To the Negro, to the white, to the farmer, to the businessman, to the Jew, to the Arab, they make their different promises. The formula is simply this: Find what people want and promise it. Devise any program and promise it to them, and then you can come into mastery over them. They become all things to all men. They operate on the principle that we are all prisoners of our immediate environment and our self-interest. With the promise to fulfil every man's self-interest, they make him a slave.

This is communism—a counterfeit and antithesis of Christianity, all evil, wearing the mask of half-truths, and marching to conquer the world! It is as the Apostle Paul said: "We are up against the unseen power that controls this dark world, and spiritual agents from the very headquarters of evil."

A New Direction

If we are to do effective battle against this enemy as a nation, it will take more than a strong military. First, our national policy in international affairs must take a new direction. Too long has expediency and inconsistency characterized our dealings with other nations. The United States has talked one way and acted another. While talking democracy and freedom, we have given military and financial support to dictators who ruthlessly denied to their people every freedom that we cherish.

Since the end of World War II, the United States has spent the fantastic sum of $85.8 billion in foreign aid. Much of this spending has been marked by ineptitude and even stupidity. In the last six years the Russians have spent only $5.6 billion on foreign aid in comparison. But they have stretched their dollars so as to convince the world that communism is the friend of all peoples who desire freedom from colonialism and dictatorship and that the United States is their enemy. I commend to you William Lederer's book *A Nation of Sheep* for a shocking, documented report on our tragic blundering in this respect.

Here is only a partial list of the dictators we have supported: Franco, a ruthless dictator, has received a billion U. S. tax dollars in economic aid and $410 million for his military.

Portugal, another dictatorship, has received $68.6 million in economic assistance and over five times that much in military aid.

We have continued the bloody Trujillo Regime in the Dominican Republic with $2.7 million in economic aid and $6.3 million in military aid. During one year, when the son, who is now dictator, was in military school in the United States, we granted Trujillo $1.5 million in U. S. tax aid. Yet his son spent a million dollars that year as a playboy student on seven servants and a plush apartment, a yacht, gala Hollywood parties, and lavish gifts to actresses that he dated. And he had a wife and six children at home at this time!

Is it any wonder we are short on friends among the poverty-stricken masses of Latin America? Today, the Trujillo Family owns half the land, all the media of communication—radio, television, newspapers—all the banks, finance companies, and more than 60 per cent of the businesses in the Republic. And still we continue to funnel millions in aid to the Dominican dictatorship.

Saudi Arabia has received $41 million in economic aid. Corruption and waste has known no limit in the foreign aid poured into Korea, Laos, and Viet Nam. But perhaps the most glaring example of the inconsistency between our profession and practice has been in Cuba. The United States spent more than $41 million keeping the dictator Batista in office. We became identified with tyranny, mass murder, and the ruthless denial of human freedoms that characterized his regime. Now communism is credited with bringing "freedom" to the oppressed Cuban people.

The crux of the matter is simply this: We cannot talk about freedom as desirable for ourselves and support tyranny elsewhere. We do not strengthen democracy by propping up, with military and financial aid, those regimes that deny its principles. If we are to meet the challenge of communism, we must carry our campaign to the little people. We must have a national policy and a foreign aid program that will give help to the little people everywhere as they struggle against tyranny for freedom, for self-determination, and for the inherent rights of free men.

A New Dynamic

Second, our motives, national and personal, must take on a new dynamic. Too long have we been motivated by dollar diplomacy. We must be moved to action by a real concern for the dispossessed, the hungry, and the politically and economically enslaved. We must stretch out hands to help without expecting anything in return. The Youth Peace Corps is a step in this direction. We are asking young people to go to the far corners of the earth and live with the little people. With kindness, help, and understanding, we would show them that a new world awaits through the door of love, freedom, and democracy.

The Peace Corps is not an untried idea. It is an enlargement of the Christian mission program. Such men as Albert Schweitzer in Africa, the late Tom Dooley in Laos, Frank Laubach with his world literacy program, and Larry Mellon with his hospital in Haiti are expressions of this distinctive Christian dynamic. The ten thousand Peace Corps workers will supplement 33,460 American missionaries who are already working in 145 countries. The training to be given in the Peace Corps is patterned after the highly successful Methodist system of training 125 young people each year for three years of Christian service overseas.

In such a program, we will be getting back to the source of the real power and greatness of our Christian civilization. As the Galilean sent men out to teach, heal, and proclaim the kingdom of God, so we are at last going to the people of the world to help them. And we are motivated by a new *dynamic* that stems from our Christian faith. Of course, this program is but as a drop of ink in an ocean of water. But it is a beginning in the right direction, the beginning of an effective answer to communism.

A New Dedication

Finally, in order to achieve this new direction and new dynamic as a nation, our personal lives must take on a new dedication to Christ and his cause. The ultimate weapon against communism will not be a missile launched across the ocean with pinpoint accuracy, or a satellite hurled into orbit carrying a death ray triggered by push buttons, or a missile-bearing, atomic submarine.

World communism is not an organized military machine. World communism is not a nationalistic movement such as characterized Hitler's, Mussolini's, or Japan's assaults on the world. As world communism marches, armies riding in tanks or planes do not cross national borders and take countries by force. Russians did not invade Cuba to establish communism there. Cubans took Cuba for communism. Russian troops are not quartered in Venezuela, but thousands of Venezuelan students in the Central University of Caracas rioted against their government recently. Russians did not paint the communist symbols and slogans I saw on the walls in Buenos Aires. They were painted by Argentine communists.

Communism is not an army but an *idea*. The only answer to an idea is a *counteridea*. You can bayonet men as they march over the hill, but *you cannot bayonet an idea on the march*. You can wipe out a city's population with a nuclear bomb, but you cannot destroy an idea with an atomic blast. You cannot drive darkness from the room with a broomstick.

You must bring in the light. Even so, the only effective answer to the darkness of communism is the light of Jesus Christ. The ultimate weapon against the idea of communism is the counter-idea of Christianity!

Here is where we must start in our battle with communism. There must be an old-fashioned revival of genuine, fervent, zealous belief in God as maker, creator, and ruler of this universe; a faith in the Bible as the revealed Word of God; a personal surrender to Jesus Christ as the Son of God and saviour of the world; and a dedication of our total selves to his church as the organized expression of the ministry of Christ in the world today. From this experience will issue forth a vital Christianity that will cause us to be sensitive to the physical and spiritual needs of men, to wage a relentless war against social and economic injustices and evil everywhere, and to sacrifice our time, money, and even our lives.

A militant minority has often changed the course of human history. Alexander the Great conquered the world with an army of 35,000. Genghis Khan conquered the world with 200,000 men. Tamerlane conquered the world with 230,000. The Communists took Russia with 40,000. Yet add the numbers of men in all the armies of all the world conquerors in all history, and you have an army considerably smaller than the vast army of Christian men and women who will stand as Sunday school teachers in the churches of the Southern Baptist denomination alone on the next Lord's Day. They will constitute a vast army of 700,000 leaders teaching Christian truth in a Sunday school that has three and a half million pupils present of the seven million enrolled. But add together all the teachers in all the Sunday schools of all denominations, and you have a number in excess of four and a half million, a corps of Christian *officers* larger than the *soldier* army of all the Communist countries of the world, Russia and her satellites, combined. What a force! What a power! J. Edgar Hoover has described it as "the power to turn the world upside down."[2]

A man enthusiastically told his pastor, "I have just joined an anticommunist organization, and you should join with us in the fight!"

The pastor answered frankly, "I already have.   In fact, I have been an active member of an anticommunist organization for thirty-five years." And he pointed to the church on the corner. Today, the church of Jesus Christ stands as the ultimate defense against communism, and vital New Testament Christianity is the only ultimate weapon that will defeat communism.

3. The Roman Road to Ruin

THE judgment of God is at times immediate and cataclysmic. God both judged and destroyed ancient Babylon in one night of violent retribution. A reveling monarch had gathered a thousand guests to feast and toast the glories of the empire. Babylon's armies had conquered the world. Her scientists, mathematicians, and astrologers were unmatched in intellectual and cultural achievements. Her hanging gardens were one of the Seven Wonders of the ancient world. Her capital city was an impregnable, walled bastion of military strength.

Suddenly, a ghostly, bodiless hand wrote in scrawling letters across the wall of the royal banquet hall: "Mene, Mene, Tekel Upharsin." Terror gripped the heart of King Belshazzar as the prophet Daniel translated the strange words, "Thou art weighed in the balances, and art found wanting." In a matter of hours, an invader had diverted the water of the Euphrates and marched in under the city wall by the dry river bed. Mighty Babylon fell amid the din of clashing arms and the shriek of the dying. Jackals now howl in the desert wastes that mark her ruins, and wild birds nest in her rubble. In one swift stroke God ushered another of man's vaunted civilizations down the road to the graveyard of nations.

Babylonian Judgment

Is a Babylonian judgment imminent for America? "The

23

handwriting on the wall of five continents now tells us that the day of Judgment is at hand." So states William Voght in his book *Road to Survival*.

"I predict that the generation in which you and I live is the last generation upon earth." Thus wrote H. G. Wells in *Mind at the End of Its Tether* just before he died.

"To one endowed with a historical perspective, it must be clear that we are at the end of world history as we know it," said Professor Albert Webber in *Farewell to European History*.

"The stable characteristics of the past 6,000 years of civilized history are being changed and are falling apart" is the seasoned observation of historian Arnold J. Toynbee, as quoted in the *New York Times*.

Thoughtful men are not only saying that judgment is at hand, but they are also prophesying God's immediate retribution in the form of cataclysmic annihilation.   Dr. Edgar Adrian, former president of the British Scientific Society, said that man has now reached the point where he *can* push a button and destroy the entire world. The armed camps of the East and West bristle with stockpiles of armaments, jet planes, missiles, nuclear warheads, spying satellites, and atomic submarines. We are told that every major city in the United States is not more than seven minutes from total destruction at any hour of the day or night as the Russian fleet of missile-bearing, atomic submarines prowls the Atlantic and the Pacific and Communist bases are established in Cuba.

We are terrified with the prospect that a finger could flick a switch on a control panel, and thirty million Americans would be killed or mortally wounded in the first twenty-four hours of the nuclear holocaust that would erupt. We are told that a mad dictator, or a trigger-happy lieutenant in a jet fighter, or a nervous communications officer misreading the blips on a radar screen—any one of these could be that one man to start World War III.

It could well be that God's judgment will come thus upon

us, as with Babylon—swift, cataclysmic, and final. But because it has not yet come, or does not soon come in this way, is no sign that God's judgment has been withheld, or that his hand of retribution has been stayed. Our immediate preservation is no proof that God has given us his divine approval. Judgment and retribution are not always simultaneous in the divine process. Sometimes God's judgments are ground out slowly on the millstones of the centuries. Of the twenty-six recorded civilizations of man on this earth, only a few have fallen in as violent a manner as Babylon. Being weighed in the balances and found wanting, they just slowly faded away into oblivion.

The Roman Road to Ruin

When Rome fell, she did not fall with the dignity you would expect of a grand and mighty empire. Babylon fell violently and dramatically in a night, while Rome slid quietly to obscurity on skids worn smooth by decades of moral decay. In our hysterical fear of communism, in the mad, nuclear-armament race, and in our military preparedness for self-preservation, we have overlooked the subtle powers of destruction that are already leading our nation down the Roman road to ruin. At the present time, internal decay and moral rot is a far greater threat to our nation than external conquest. Forces are at work within our society that are the prime destroyers of the good that man has done. The evils that toppled the Roman Empire and other nations will likewise destroy America.

In the *Decline and Fall of the Roman Empire*, the famous historian Gibbons set forth five reasons why Rome fell. There is a shocking similarity to the way Rome fell and prevailing conditions in our nation today.

The first reason Gibbons gave for the fall of Rome was *the steady increase in sexual immorality, divorce, and the breakup of the Roman home*. How do we weigh by this measurement?

I shall not ask the pulpit for a comment. Too often we are

calloused to the formal judgment of the church. Rather I call
to the witness stand the eminent sociologist Dr. Pitirim A.
Sorokin, of Harvard University. He describes the moral environment in America as one of sex anarchy.[1] He lists nine
categories of evidence sustaining this point. They include:

1. Premarital and extramarital sex relations have increased; this was reconfirmed by Kinsey and other scientifically
reliable surveys.

2. Traffic in pornographic literature has greatly increased.
Post office officials estimate that fifty million pieces of pornographic
literature are mailed every year to teen-agers. This is a multimillion
dollar business. Look at the average newsstand. Notice the number
of "yellow dog" papers, the scandal magazines that make a business
of uncovering salacious stories on celebrities. It is estimated that
fifty new titles a year are being introduced to the market. Notice
also the large number of slick men's magazines filled with nudes
in full color and featuring stories of sex exploits and drinking
bouts. More than fifty different magazines of this type are being
published today. Postal regulations classify these magazines as
pornographic literature, so they are distributed from the publisher
to the newsdealer by private truck.

3. The absorption of the public's interest in sex novels, sex
songs, sex plays, and sex movies has ballooned. The 1960 Academy Award picture was *The Apartment,* a story of the illicit sex
exploits of business men. The Oscar for the best actress went to
Liz Taylor for her role as a prostitute in *Butterfield 8.* Of the ten
big-money Hollywood productions of 1960, six had a prostitute
as the heroine. Don't blame Hollywood! Movie moguls are not
crusading for morality or immorality. They just look at the cash
in the box office till. They produce the kind of pictures the
American public pays to see.

4. Divorce and redivorce has increased. A Moslem may divorce his wife simply by saying three times, "I divorce you." We
decry a society and religion which tolerates such immorality and
irresponsibility. Yet our divorce mills continue to grind out one
divorce for every three marriages.

5. The number of desertions are mounting. A million men
have walked away from their wives and families to disappear,

taking the poor man's route to divorce. A hundred thousand more men will walk off this year and disappear.

As a result of this sex anarchy, the basic unit of our society, the home, is threatened. Three hundred thousand children are affected by divorce every year. Dean Kenneth D. Johnson, of Columbia University, said, "Imagine 300,000 children stricken annually by infantile paralysis! Yet the chances of this number of children being crippled emotionally by divorce is far greater than the chances of physical crippling by polio."[2]

With sex anarchy and broken homes, involving hundreds of thousands of children as the backwash of the divorce court, emotionally and morally crippled for life, our society is steadily propelled down the Roman road to ruin.

The second reason that Gibbons gave for the decline of the Roman Empire was *higher and higher taxes, until the load became unbearable, while officials of the Empire continued to spend public funds with reckless indifference.*

There is a simple law of economics that even a Harvard egghead cannot change. If I make $50.00 a week and spend $49.00, I will save a little and in time have a nest egg. Though my savings are small, I will be economically solvent. But if I make $50.00 a week and spend $51.00 a week, there is no escape. I will become insolvent and bankrupt. This is true individually and true collectively, in business or in a nation. Ponder what deficit spending and increased bureaucracy has done to our economy. These figures are staggering!

One dollar out of every $10.00 collected in Federal taxes goes to *pay the interest* on our national debt.

The number of Federal employees has increased seven times in thirty years.

The cost of the Federal Government operation in the four years 1956—60 exceeded the total cost of the Federal Government during its first 152 years of operation. The total cost of the Federal Government in the period 1789—1940 was $167 billion. The proposed Eisenhower budget for 1961 was

$41.8 billion. The Kennedy administration projected an increase of $2.1 billion immediately upon inauguration.

We look in vain for a turning in this road. The platforms of both parties in the national election promised little hope. Both candidates campaigned on promises to a variety of special-interest groups that the Government would do more than ever before for them. And we the voters have made it so!

Ask the farmer, "Do you want socialized farming?" He responds with a caustic, "No!" But ask him if he wants to give up his government crop support, and again he says, "No."

Ask the laborer, "Do you want higher taxes and government operation of industry?" He says, "No!" But ask him to give up a guaranteed minimum wage, increased social security benefits, government and industrial hospitalization, a guaranteed annual wage, increased and lengthened unemployment benefits, and he will resist.

Ask the businessman what to do. He will tell you, "Cut down government spending with the farmer; cut out government interference with labor." But business howls at any proposal to cut down the government subsidy to airlines, or to eliminate the tax write offs for industrial expansion, or to discard the special tax benefits for "reserve depletion" to the oil industry or the oyster industry.

Ask the national Chamber of Commerce what to do. They say, "Cut down the government spending." But notice how the local chamber of commerce works to get a hand in the pork barrel and capture every Federal-financed highway program, housing project, or defense contract possible to boost the local economy.

The truth is that we are all guilty of looking to the Federal Government to solve our personal problems. More and more, we depend on a central government with increased authority to care for us as we become less responsible and less resourceful at the local and individual levels. Thus we go on down the Roman road to ruin trying to spend ourselves rich, like an alcoholic trying to drink himself sober.

The third reason for the decline of Rome was *a mad desire for excitement leading to all sorts of moral extravagances which finally engulfed the Empire and destroyed it.* Rome went on a pleasure binge! The wild, insatiable desire for excitement, thrills, and exotic activity found expression in the arena, in the chariot races, and the gladitorial contests. The same frenetic pattern is obvious in our society.

Gambling is at an all-time high with a take of millions every week. It cuts across all of life. The Catholic Church raises money with bingo. The civic club raffles a car for charity. Office employees make up a football pool. Bookies are always on hand to take a bet on a "fly-ball percentage," a "buck on a card of winners," or "$2.00 on a nag to win, place, or show." Most major cities have a numbers racket called the "bug." The take is millions in pennies and nickels. It is said to be a $60 million racket in Chicago alone. A Miami law student reportedly ran a numbers racket that grossed $600,000 in one year, according to the Kefauver investigation.

Sportsmanship has ceased to be the end in sports for many people. It is now big business, with everything else secondary to getting a winner. Football scholarships and subsidies overshadow the academic interest and concern of many universities.

Even the teen-ager is looking for a new "kick" in life. In Chicago, a million dollar dope ring was discovered operating in the high schools. It was found that a dope ring was operating in Fort Mitchell, Kentucky, selling marijuana cigarets, commonly called reefers, to school children. The first was sold for 10¢, the second for 25¢, the third for 50¢, the fourth for $1.00, and then all thereafter sold for $5.00 when the young person was already hooked!

Rock-and-roll dancing—if dancing is the proper word to describe its jerking, twisting, squirming contortions—is but another facet of the same problem. Teen-agers reflect the mood of their parents and the climate of the society in which they live. Elvis Presley, appearing in Oklahoma City, required police protection to keep a wild, screaming crowd of teen-age girls from mobbing him. A reporter had his clothes torn from him, as the girls shouted, "Let me touch *him;* he touched Elvis!" Thirteen million Presley records and $21 million worth of Presley-endorsed products were sold in one year attesting to his popularity.

These are the shallow roots of our society. We are afflicted with what psychologists call activism. We have ceased *being* and are driven by a mad compulsion to *doing.* Drive, drive! Do, do! Go, go! Thrill, thrill! Live it up! This is the tempo of our times, as it was in Rome—a mad desire for excitement —and all kinds of moral extravagances.

The fourth cause of the fall of the Roman Empire was *an increased political pressure for armaments with blind disregard for the destructive element building up inside the Empire.* We have a blind, hysterical fear of frontal attack by Russia. We are pitting all our national resources and strength in an arms race against Russia and communism. More money was spent by the United States for military defenses in 1961, $43 billion, than was spent by the Federal Government for all expenses between 1789 to 1918. Defense now takes 57 per cent of the United States' budget. Yet we blindly disregard the internal rot and corruption eating at the vitals of society.

The business world in 1960 was rocked when seven top, electrical-company executives were sentenced to Norristown Prison, in Pennsylvania. These men, whose annual salaries were written in five and six figures, worked for thirty cents a day at the side of common crooks. Their companies paid millions in fines while these men served time because the Justice Department convicted them of participating in a giant conspiracy of price fixing, collusion, and cheating the public out of multiple millions of dollars. In the trial, the defense attorney pleaded, "These men have done nothing wrong. It is a way of life. Everybody is doing it!" This is the tragedy. This is a way of life for business. Anything goes to make a fast dollar.

Harry Bridges, Jimmy Hoffa, and their kind disgrace the labor movement with indescribable dishonesty.

The academic world was staggered in 1958 by a survey showing 75 per cent of the college seniors admitted cheating and that only 13 per cent felt a cheating student was basically dishonest.

The public was shocked by the disclosure that many television quiz programs were rigged. Disc jockeys were taking payola. We applauded when some of the brave participants appeared before Senate investigators and confessed their dishonesty. Yet when the Gallup poll made a survey of public opinion, it revealed that most of the people in our country saw nothing wrong in rigged shows and payola!

Former President Herbert Hoover, speaking in Des Moines, Iowa, said that there is "a cancerous growth of intellectual dishonesty in public life. . . . These evils have defeated nations many times in history."

Remember the Chinese Wall? It was two thousand miles long, built as a barricade on the western border of China to keep out the invader. For centuries, the Wall successfully defended their land. But one day an enemy bribed a dishonest gatekeeper; the invaders filed through the door at midnight and conquered China. The ultimate defense of any nation lies, not in its walls or armaments, but in the morality, integrity, and character of its people.

The fifth reason for the fall of Rome was *a decline in religion and a withholding of support from character-building institutions.*

Here is our door of escape! Even as Rome fell because of a turning from religion, so we can be saved by a return to religion. By a revival of vital Christianity, we can turn from national suicide and an imminent destiny in the graveyard of nations. The New Testament church can put back into our society the character and moral fiber to save us.

What is happening to our nation? Simply stated, we are fast becoming a pagan nation. The moral and spiritual foundations of our society are crumbling because great geographical areas and population concentrations of unchurched people have developed. Unreached and untouched by a vital New Testament witness, these hard cores of paganism have become centers of influence in our society and have set the pattern for our nation as a whole.

How has this happened? Two factors are evident. They involve population shifts and the social and moral disintegration that comes with the large-scale displacement of people as they are uprooted from stable communities and are cut off from the moral influence of established churches and other character-building institutions.

First, there has been a shift from a rural to urban society. In 1790, 3 per cent of the population lived in the city. In 1960, 46 per cent of our population lived in cities, and we are moving to the city at a rate of a million more a year. Because of the rapid growth of our cities and urban suburbs, and because these new areas remain largely unchurched, a pagan city culture has developed which is characterized by a disregard for the old standards of the rural church community, such as Sabbath observance, abstinence, modesty, morality, and church loyalty.

Second is the population shift out of the deep, Bible-belt South into the other regions of our nation. During the past ten years, 81.9 per cent of these rural counties lost in population.

These great population concentrations in the East, North, and West are pagan mission fields similar to the frontier mission fields in the early development of our country. Then the pioneers rolled westward so rapidly that churches were unable to keep up with this population shift. The pioneer West was unchurched and thus lawless, violent, and immoral. This held true until it was penetrated by Christian missionaries and ministers and until the stabilizing moral influence of a local church was brought to bear on the life of the frontier community.

In the East, Paul James, pastor of the Manhattan Baptist Church, said there are seven million unchurched people in New York City alone. There are more unchurched people in this one city than in six of the largest, deep-South states combined. All the persons in attendance in all the synagogues, churches, and cathedrals of New York City could be seated in the taxicabs on Sunday morning. There are forty-five million people in the ten-state area of New England.

In the five-state area of the Midwest centering in Colorado, 75 per cent of the population is unchurched. To the Far West is California where one-sixth of the total population gain for the United States during 1950-60 took place. Eighty per cent of these people are unchurched. They represent a core of paganism no different from Africa or Japan as far as vital New Testament Christianity is concerned.

If we are to save our nation and turn it to God, we must save these people. Sociologists say that "as goes the city, so goes a society." In the last presidential election, we were reminded of the fact that five states, California and four eastern states, could elect a president. In other words, it makes little difference in national policy or destiny what the Bible-belt South might do—politically, morally, or spiritually. The moral and spiritual destiny of the nation ultimately depends upon whether or not these great population centers are Christianized!

Furthermore, if these geographical areas and population centers are to be reached for Christ, it will take a revitalized Christian witness on the part of many churches. Not all denominations and churches still have the spiritual vitality to meet this challenge. Even in these booming population areas, some old-line denominations and churches, long established there, are giving up and pulling out to abandon the city because of the problems and difficulties encountered. Dr. Paul James reports that one denomination in New York City has dissolved fifty-four congregations and merged forty-two others with other churches in the past few years.

New Vision and Vitality

I believe there is a new vision in our churches today to meet this challenge. In 1956, Dr. C. C. Warren, then president of the Southern Baptist Convention, led that denomination to launch a program for building 30,000 new missions, preaching stations, and churches by 1964. Recently, he reported to the Executive Committee of the denomination that already more than 11,000 of these new stations had been established. Other denominations have joined them, and they are penetrating these areas with the gospel.

I also believe that there is a new open vitality in our Christianity and church life for the first time in generations. Mass evangelism has come back into its own. We have the spiritual phenomena of Billy Graham speaking to the nation as a voice from God. There has been a return to simple Bible faith and a renewed interest in Bible study. For example, Dr. W. L. Howse, head of the Division of Education for the Baptist Sunday School Board, stated that seven million pupils are now enrolled in Southern Baptist Sunday schools. This is the largest group in the history of Christendom ever to gather for a regular systematic study of the Word of God. The skepticism of thirty years ago that came out of the universities and theological schools of Germany has been cast aside. In many denominations, a return to biblical theology and to fundamental doctrine is being manifested. The cause of mission advance, evangelism, and outreach for people has become the primary concern of major denominations.

I believe that America can be saved from the hand of God's judgment. I believe every church and every denomination can have a part in this spiritual and moral recovery. Our nation will regain her place of greatness in the world when we give the same priority to moral armament that we now give to the military. We must recapture the *Pilgrim's* love for freedom and individual responsibility; the *Puritan's* zeal for morality and integrity; and the *pioneer's* spirit to conquer the new spiritual and moral frontiers before us.

In the Allied invasion of France during World War II, a chaplain idly asked a sergeant, "Building a new world?" The soldier answered, "No, Chaplain, we are tearing down the old. It is your job to build it new." Military, diplomatic, and political forces can only tear down the old or police the status quo. If we have a new world, a new nation, or even a new community, *we must build it—you and I—through the church of the living Lord.*

"In the beginning God created . . ."
(Genesis 1:1).

4. Our Lost Reverence

ON April 12, 1961, earthbound man broke his shackles and invaded space. At 9:05 A.M. Yuri Gagarin, stocky twenty-seven-year-old cosmonaut blasted off in a five-ton, Russian spaceship named *Vostok,* or *"East."* A multi-stage rocket hurled the satellite at speeds upwards of 25,000 miles per hour out of the earth's atmosphere and into an egg-shaped orbit. Gagarin circled the earth at a distance varying from 109.5 miles to 187.75 miles in a total time of 89.1 minutes, and then safely landed from his craft. The achievement of this son of an almost illiterate carpenter may well write his name in history beside those of Columbus, Magellan, and Lindbergh.

From this scientific beachhead, man expects to push on in the total conquest of outer space. Dr. Wernher von Braun, America's leading rocket expert, has predicted that within our lifetime trips to the moon will be commonplace, the exploration of Mars and Venus will have been completed, and expeditions will be underway to make a landing on Saturn, Jupiter, and their satellites.[1]

Dr. Percival Lowell, founder of Flagstaff Observatory, believes that the fine markings on Mars, commonly called canals, are the work of intelligent beings.[2] If he is correct, some of us living today may experience the thrilling moment when earthman establishes communication with these intelligent creatures inhabiting Mars. Dr. Cyrill Stanyukovich, of the Soviet Academy of Sciences, predicts that man will develop rockets capable of traveling at the speed of light, 186,000 miles per second.[3] They will make possible the exploration of outer space billions of miles beyond our solar system.

Thus, what was yesterday's fantasy, found only in the Buck Rogers comic strip, has become today's destiny for earthman. Man crawled slowly through the Stone Age, plodded through the Bronze Age, walked through the Iron Age, and on August 6, 1945, when the first atomic bomb was dropped on Hiroshima, plunged into the Atomic Age. And now we find ourselves rocket propelled into another age, the Space Age.

While the penetration of space is a dramatic demonstration of man's rapid advance, an even more staggering, but less apparent, advance is being made in man's accumulation of knowledge. From the minutest recesses of the atom to the farthest expanses of the universe, man is today discovering and classifying new information at a phenomenal rate.

John McPartland has suggested a formulation of the speed at which scientific knowledge is being developed.[4] The formula is the same as that for the surface of an expanding sphere; human knowledge is increasing as the square of the radial increases. We are acquiring as much new information each two years as we acquired in the total of human history up to now. Within five years that two-year span will decrease to one year; within ten years it will diminish to three months. This projection was made in 1952! Add the factor of new developments since then, such as the electrical computer and the mechanical brain, and the forecast is most conservative.

Undoubtedly, we are living in mankind's greatest age. Surpassing anything the world has ever known, including Christopher Columbus's discovery and penetration of a new world, these days of expanding knowledge are filled with more potential for change than any other age of man.

Lost Reverence and Science

These spectacular achievements have been as a sip of heady wine for earth-bound man. He is overwhelmed with his ability and intoxicated with his self-importance. The creature believes he has become the creator. A secondary role in the universe is no longer satisfying to his new ego. To be made in the image of God is not enough. Some dare to suggest that man's ultimate destiny is to become God himself!

Sir Julian Huxley, noted British biologist and humanist, has prophesied that man is destined to outgrow both religion and God. Sir Julian said that both are a part of life's evolutionary processes, and that God and religion are destined to be left behind. The spiritual is only a phase of man's development.

Ben Hecht wrote in a popular magazine that we have outgrown the God of the Old and New Testaments and the Christian God of the pre-Space Age.[5] He contends that the revelation of the telescope and the microscope is too much for Jesus and his limited followers who wrote the New Testament. The Bible is obsolete and incomplete. "Your preachers of the Space Age will not be the traditional clerics but the astronauts who will come back from their interplanetary explorations and be our teachers about the new God of the Space Age."

This then is the issue we face: Is science our new messiah? What is the role of science in the organized life of mankind? Communism long since has answered this question. Today, the Soviets look to science as the one Messiah that will give ultimate victory to their materialistic system. Khrushchev's wild boast that Gagarin's flight "contains a new triumph of Lenin's ideas, a confirmation of the correctness of Marxist-Leninist teaching" thus takes on awesome significance as the god of science moves them closer to their objective of world domination.

Can a spiritual God save us as a nation, or must we look to science for survival? There are those who say that science is interested in real things and religion deals only with that which is unreal. Science is moving ahead and religion is retreating. Science is concerned with this world while religion is hypnotized with dreams of another world. What is the relevance of the Bible, the church, traditional Christian faith, and the spiritual for Space Age man? Shall we reverence only that which is material? Are the only relevant values in life to be those that enhance the physical well-being of man? Is science a *goal* or a *god?*

An Old Problem

These questions have haunted the Western world since the first, successful atomic test at Alamogordo, New Mexico. Indeed, these questions have troubled men for generations.

A century ago, on November 24, 1859, the conflict between scientism and religion was brought into sharp focus by a book so controversial and anticipated that on the day of publication every copy was sold by 3:00 P.M. Thus Charles Darwin's *Origin of the Species* made an unmatched record in publishing history and a lasting impression on the minds of men. From Darwin's thesis, Huxley and others concluded that man was the latest arrival in a long progression of mechanical evolution. Man's true origin, therefore, was not in any creative act of a benevolent God. Man had his beginning from a single life cell in inorganic slime, washed up on a bleak, gray beach of a primeval sea billions of years ago. The further conclusion was that "this is not *God's* world, but *man's* world."

Sigmund Freud, the psychologist, carried the thesis still further. He concluded that the psychic man is not a spiritual being made in the image of God, but merely a physical being made only in the image of the lower animal that produced him. Then followed the behavioristic psychology of Pavlov, which explained man simply as a bundle of conditioned reflexes. Control man's environment and you will make a perfect man! Behaviorism cut across all lines. Educational psychology became enamored with it. Even religious education applied some concepts of behaviorism to its philosophy in the development of the Christian nurture theory.

Horace Bushnell was the spokesman of this school which assumed that if a child were reared in the proper environment, he would automatically be a Christian, need never be lost, and thus need never be saved. Evangelism was termed a mop to clean up only when Christian nurture had failed. Everyone sought to be an amatuer psychologist, tossing into conversation such sophisticated phrases as Oedipus complex, father fixation, inhibitions, and frustrations. Troubled people turned from the Bible, prayer, and worship to beat a path to the psychiatrists, who probed the depths of their subconscious minds to give them release from guilt feelings, anxiety, and frustration and deliver to them peace of mind.

And now man has hurled a satellite into space! As the electronic "beeps" and "burps" come back from the cosmos, and we see a gleaming, man-made star plunging through the heavens, we have rewritten Scripture to read, "The heavens declare the glory of, not *God,* but *man."* First Darwin, then Freud, and now man is in the star-making business. Surely, God is finished!

Competitors or Companions?

But God is not finished. Let us bring the issue into focus with three affirmations.

First, biblical Christianity is here to stay! The faith that culminated historically in the supreme revelation of God in Christ reconciling the world unto himself on the cross and the divinely inspired account of this revelation, the Bible, *has* and *will* endure, supremely adequate for man's every spiritual need. The promise still stands: "The word of the Lord endureth for ever" (1 Peter 1:25). In every generation, vain and boastful men have attacked Christianity and the authority of the Word of God. It is said that hundreds of birds die nightly by beating their wings against the light in the upraised hand of the Statue of Liberty in New York harbor. The caretaker gathers up the broken bodies scattered around the base each morning. And the light still shines. Even so the Caretaker of eternity gathers up the broken lives of the foolish critics who have hurled themselves against the light of the Word. As they fall into oblivion, the light continues to shine.

Second, science is here to stay. Gandhi traveled throughout India drinking goat's milk, wearing sandals and a cotton sheet, and carrying a miniature spinning wheel. He said to the people, "The mass-producing machine is a symbol of Western civilization. Beware of their civilization; resist their machines and stay close to nature." We cannot travel Gandhi's road. We cannot close our lives to the discoveries of science. Nor can we close our minds to the search for new truth.

Christianity should never say, "Do not investigate! Ask no questions! Never search, never seek for new truth." To say this is in itself a denial of a facet of the image of God implanted in man. God has given man an insatiable thirst for knowledge, a compulsion for advancement. An upward reach is in our very nature. To deny or suppress this upward thrust intellectually, scientifically, or spiritually is to deny the One who implanted this godly drive within us.

Third, religion and science are not hostile competitors but companions in truth. If one says, "I find an irreconcilable conflict between intellect and faith, between science and Christianity," then that person is lacking in a proper understanding of the true purpose, either of science or of Christianity.

Let a contemporary scientist speak on this subject. Dr. Warren Weaver, former head of the Department of Mathematics at the University of Wisconsin and chairman of the Board of the American Association for the Advancement of Science, stated, "Every new discovery of science is a further revelation of God. Scientists are precisely the persons who believe in the unbelievable, the essentially undefinable. I believe that the Bible is the purest revelation we have of the nature and goodness of God."[6] Dr. Wernher von Braun, writing for *This Week* magazine, declared that his life was predicated on two principles, faith and scientific reasoning![7] Notice the order—faith is first!

Science and religion are not in conflict. They are not *competitors, but companions,* in truth. They are two totally different views of the same truth. I hold in my hand a new nickel. It is one coin, but it has two sides. The appearance of the coin depends on which side is viewed. From one side, I see a building, Monticello, drawn in lines, dimensions, and proportions. From the other side, I see a man's face. Two sides of one coin! Thus science looks at one side of the coin of truth and sees measurement, design, and physical characteristics, like this building. But religion takes an interpretive look at the other side of the same coin of truth and sees the face of a Person. He sees God in the truth. The apparent conflict between science and religion is often based on a misunderstanding of the viewpoint, the purpose, and the interpretation of each.

The Bible and Science

Four principles of interpretation can help resolve imagined conflicts between the Bible and science.

First, the Bible is not a book of science, but a book of religious fundamentals and truths. The Bible does not propose to give the scientific answers, but the religious and spiritual answers, to man's questions. He who would make of the Bible a scientific textbook or timetable misunderstands it. The Bible is the story of God's progressive revelation of himself to man —his love, his will, his principles for moral conduct, and, in Jesus Christ, his redemptive purpose for mankind. As such, the Bible is eternal and remains unchanged, ever adequate to meet the deeper needs of the human heart.

Science, on the other hand, is ever changing. The textbooks of science on my library shelf from college days are already obsolete and inadequate for my Space Age children. Science is constantly changing its concepts, its theories, and its interpretation of discoveries. At one time men thought the world rested on the back of four elephants, or was flat and floated in a sea, or was the center around which the sun revolved. Investigation brought new theories, but absolute and final scientific truth remains elusive. Scientific hypotheses and theories are always being revised. Amid this constant flux of science, the revelation of God to man in the person of Christ his Son and the Bible as the account of that revelation remains unchanged. It declares, "In the beginning God" and concludes, "I am Alpha and Omega."

Second, the Bible answers the question "why?" Science answers the question "how?" Dr. Warren Weaver explains the purpose of science.

Science tries to answer the question: "HOW?" How do cells act in the body? How do you design an airplane that can fly faster than sound? How is a molecule of insulin constructed? Science attempts to analyze how things and people and animals behave; it has no concern whether this behaviour is good or bad, is purposeful or not.[8]

Dr. Weaver continues by saying that religion answers the questions of right or wrong, of good or bad. Religion answers the question "why?" "Religion, to me is first, a guide to conduct" and, "second, it is the theory of moral meaning for our existence."

Thus we look to the Bible for the answers to questions that science does not answer, does not propose to answer, and could never answer. Why should I tell the truth? Why must there be pain and suffering in the world? Why is man on earth? Why is sin in the world? Why does man have an insatiable thirst for God? Why has God not abandoned man?

Third, the Bible recognizes progress and order in the universe and in creation. Centuries before Darwin conceived his hypothesis, the Bible had set forth the concept that the world came into existence in periods of development. The Genesis account speaks of six periods or "days." These days could well involve millions of years as scientists now tell us, for God is timeless. There is no issue between the Bible and science over the antiquity of the earth or the length of these periods.

The Bible is not a book of science setting the dates and lengths of these periods, but it is a revelation of truth that God was active in the *progressive creation* of this universe. Neither is there an issue over the fact of the development of life on earth at different levels, in a progression from lower to higher, simple to complex. The Bible sets forth this same principle: God's creative activity was progressive and purposeful.

But the Bible goes further than science. The Bible not only says that "In the beginning *God created,*" in an orderly process and in regular periods, this universe and life on it. The Bible also declares that *God is still in the world.* He has not abandoned it. He is in it, imminent and personal. He is still dealing with his creation. He did not wind up the earth as an alarm clock, set it on a shelf, and abandon it to run down.

The Bible further tells us *where this world is going.* God is not through. He is moving this earth and humanity toward an eternal destiny, the kingdom of God itself.

The Harvard astronomer Dr. Harlow Shapley has said that a purely scientific look at the world would cause one to conclude that "the earth is a grain of sand with a whiff of atmosphere and a smear of biology, plodding its way around the sun with a monotonous regularity." But the scientist, as a man of faith, finds in the Bible something to add to his scientific knowledge. One of the men closest to our Space Age discoveries General John B. Medaris, head of the United States Army Ordnance Missile Development at Huntsville, Alabama, said that for him religion and faith in the Bible answers such questions as "Who am I? Where am I going? Who and where is the authority for my life?" Religion, he said, gives purpose and direction to his life.[9]

Dr. Wernher von Braun, director of the Marshall Space Flight Center, National Aeronautics and Space Administration, said:

There are two forces which move us. One is a belief in a Last Judgment when everyone of us has to account for what we did with God's great gift of life on the earth. The other is belief in an immortal soul, a soul which will cherish the award or suffer the penalty decreed in a final judgment. In our modern world people seem to feel that science has somehow made such "religious ideas" seem untimely or old-fashioned. But I think science has a real surprise for the skeptics. Science, for instance, tells us that nothing in nature, not even the tiniest particle, can disappear without a trace. *Nature does not know extinction. All it knows is transformation.* Now, if God applies this fundamental principle to the most minute and insignificant parts of His universe, doesn't it make sense to assume that He applies it also to the masterpiece of His creation—the human soul? I think it does. And everything science has taught me—and continues to teach me—strengthens my belief in the continuity of our spiritual existence after death. Nothing disappears without a trace.[10]

Fourth, the Bible declares that the creative activity of God is both central and eternal. It is proposed that life developed from a lower to a higher form by chance variation followed by the survival of the fittest, and that the *total explanation* for life can be found in evolution. Yet Robert Clark has observed that this does not explain the ordered nature of the energy in the universe, nor the properties of the chemical elements. It does not solve the major biological differences and gives only a plausible explanation for minor biological changes.

For example, many biological structures, like functional structures, must all be there at once or they serve no purpose. A car without wheels or a tape recorder without tape is useless. Yet some would say that these many, minor component parts all came by gradual change at exactly the same time and survived by natural selection. An even greater difficulty is the problem of size. A fly the size of a dog would break its legs and a dog the size of a fly would be unable to maintain its body heat. Radically new designs would be necessary for survival. Natural selection could not survive such redesign.

The scientist today is ready to admit that more questions are raised than answered in many of the theories. Again and again, the scientist is forced back to the only logical explanation, *creation.* However, creation should not be thought of as some magical activity but an actual effort of God. The power of creativity resides even in man. He uses this power when he designs a bridge or writes a book. In the very act of creation, power goes out of a man when he does these things. Man creates by the expenditure of energy, faith, and the mind.

So do not think of God as an almighty magician. The Bible portrays God as a person, a Supreme Being, who, by forethought and care, created the world. After power went from him through this creative act, the Bible says he rested from his labors.[11] The Bible does not attempt to answer *how* he did these things. That is the realm of science. But the Bible asserts he was active in the process, and the Bible gives the most satisfying explanation philosophically and religiously as to *why* God did these things.

Those who would rule out a creative God must admit three inexplainable scientific gaps.

There is the problem of first cause. Place a hundred bricks on end, one inch apart. Push brick number 100 over, and in a chain reaction all bricks fall. As we watch brick number 1 fall, we ask, "What made it fall?"

The answer: "Simple! Brick 2 fell against it."

"What made brick 2 fall?"

"Easy! Brick 3!"

But the real question has never been answered, only postponed. It is: "What made the first brick fall when there was no other brick prior to it?"

The only answer is: "A personality entered in, exercising free will, and started the chain reaction." The mechanical evolutionist answers the question "Who made man?" by reciting a sequence: "Lower animals, fish, one-cell life, inorganic ooze, sea water, and cosmic dust." But the real question is still evaded, and remains: "What was the first cause?" There is only one answer: *In the beginning, God.*

Just as the *first* cause is a problem to those ruling out a God of creative activity, *continuing* cause also is a problem. The real issue between the Bible and any theory that rules out a creative God is not over the *sequence* of development but over the *cause* of development. Some persons would conclude that sequence proves causation. This is like the boy riding a train and eating his first banana. When the train went into a tunnel and plunged him into darkness, he concluded that the banana caused blindness! A purely mechanistic theory of evolution is guilty of this same faulty reasoning in concluding that a lower form of life *caused* a higher form, just because they were related in a time sequence. In such a conclusion, science has moved out of the realm of the observation of facts into the realm of speculation.

And science is just as awkward in the field of philosophy as religion is in the field of science. If I speak of the evolution of the automobile, I refer to the fact that the present-day automobile was developed in a series of observable steps from one design to another. But it would be absurd to conclude that the lower automobile *produced,* of itself, a higher automobile. For designers produced one and then another.

Thus science observes steps in development, but the Bible says that this life did not come in itself and of itself, but that from the beginning, God created the universe and all life in it. Christian faith declares that life came by the creative act of a personal God. Using lower materials to produce higher life, he created all by an act of his own free will, not automatic, mechanically, or by a self-contained process.

The second gap concerns the first matter. How did it come into existence? Science has observed that energy and matter can be neither destroyed nor created by natural means. The only answer is that a supernatural First Cause, God, created out of nothing the first energy and matter of this cosmos.

At this point, an interesting current hypothesis of physics concerning the nature of matter and this physical universe is worth noting. It is suggested that the basic unit of the universe (the atom) is not a bit of "stuff," or solid units, like little golf balls; but instead, it is an *event.* Something *happens,* not *is,* in a space-time continuum. Thus the electron is not a bit of stuff but an electrical charge, or burst of oscillating energy. It is not a *thing* charged with energy, but it is an event. If this is true, we might say that the world comes nearer being a great *thought* rather than a great machine, and it is essentially *spiritual* rather than material. This is one trend in scientific thought today. Such a concept would make God continually imminent in the world as the dynamic source of everything!

The third unanswerable question is the gap between the higher animals and man. Scientists can trace a pattern of design and function in physical bodies—from the fin of the fish to the hand of a man, for example. He thus explains somewhat the design of man's body as evolving from a lower design found in other life. But this cannot explain man himself! Something new is found in man, nonexistent in all other forms of life. Here is *will, moral choice, faith, conscience, capacity for worship, ability to create, and capacity for mathematics and scientific inquiry.* If man is the product of an evolutionary sequence, you would find all of these elements to a lesser degree in other forms of life. But this is not so. Man is different! As the Bible affirms, man *was created* by God—a special, unique, distinct creation.

A Faith for the Space Age

Reverent science and intelligent Christianity are not in conflict. Arguments, marked by more heat than light, will continue. But science and Christian faith are like the twin tracks of a railroad. They both must go forward together, parallel, and at the same time. Each serves a function of its own in meeting the needs of man. Each makes a distinctive contribution as man is carried along on the dual tracks toward God's goal for creation. Here is a faith for the Space Age.

This is God's world. He made it. He is still in it. He is guiding it toward a purposeful redemptive goal. With every advance of science, with every new discovery, we are overwhelmed with the great mystery of this universe. And we say in reverent awe, "The heavens declare the glory of God; and the firmament sheweth his handywork."

Man is God's creature—created by God, in the image of

God, and for fellowship with God. Unique and distinct, we belong to him.

Sin has separated us from God. The destiny of every human soul is to find God and be restored to fellowship with him.

The good news of Christianity is that God was in Christ reconciling the world to himself. Through Christ, God's creative power is still at work in the universe. Through Christ, God is creating a new humanity, with a redeemed nature and a changed character, made into his likeness to be his sons. Surpassing all that God has ever done in creating this world and life on it, he is even now working his greatest miracle, the miracle of his love and grace in the human heart. John W. Peterson said it this way:

> My Father is omnipotent,
>   And that you can't deny;
> A God of might and miracles;
>   'Tis written in the sky.
>
> It took a miracle to put the stars in place;
> It took a miracle to hang the world in space.
>   But when He saved my soul,
>   Cleansed and made me whole,
> It took a miracle of love and grace![12]

"Don't get your stimulus from wine (for there is always the danger of excessive drinking), but let the Spirit stimulate your souls" (Eph. 5:18, Phillips).

5. The Menace of Moderation

THE hard sell of the liquor industry is that the moderate drinking of beverage alcohol has given to millions of Americans a new, relaxed, enjoyable, supremely happy way of life. Men of distinction "testify" to this. In national magazines four-color pictures of roses, sports events, hunting safaris, and elegantly dressed men sitting on white horses portray the luxurious living that liquor lends. A foamy glass of beer is poured right into our living room, via television, assuring us that "beer belongs."

Promoted to the tune of $300 million a year in newspaper and magazine advertising and $350 million more in radio and television advertising, the liquor industry perpetuates this fraud that the moderate use of legal liquor enriches life and blesses society. The true facts of their exploitation for profit of man's weakness is disguised with conscienceless deceit. Any news item or editorial piece that refers to drunkenness or reflects on the alcoholic industry produces a strong reaction in the advertising department, and the news media soon learns who butters their bread.

The Big Lie

Hitler coined the phrase "the Big Lie." It was his oft-repeated strategy. The bigger the lie, the more there are who will believe it. Repeat it often enough and people will believe anything. *Pageant* magazine, in an article "The Big Lie About Moderate Drinking," charged the liquor industry with this same strategy.

This is their Big Lie—"There is *no harm in moderate drinking*. Do not prohibit drinking; just teach moderation." But who can draw the line between moderate drinking and alcoholism? Several years ago, a book *The Lost Weekend,* which describes the problems of an alcoholic, became a best seller. Hollywood filmed the story. Ray Milland, as the alcoholic, graphically revealed the tragic sufferings of the compulsive drinker.

Seagram's Distilleries published a full-page news advertisement to counteract the bad publicity from the picture. They piously declared, "We have always said that there are some men who should not drink." But here is the unsolved problem which the liquor industry ignores without conscience: *Which man should not drink?* Thousands of tests have shown that it cannot be predicted who among moderate drinkers will become an alcoholic. Neither science nor Seagram's can tell you *which man* should not drink.

We know that as fifteen people start down the road of moderate drinking, two will become confirmed alcoholics. Three more will become problem drinkers. Five out of fifteen! One out of every three are cursed and damned by moderate drinking. As Upton Sinclair said, "I would be a fool to keep in my house a dog that would bite and maim one out of every three visitors."

An advertisement taken from *Life* magazine shows a daring, iceboat racer taking his chances on Greenwood Lake. It advertises a brand of eight-year-old whiskey. The ad is labeled: "It is great to take chances—but not on your bourbon." This is the Big Lie—the chance is not in the *boat* but in the *bottle*. This bottle is a gun; it is loaded with fifteen bullets. Two of these bullets can curse you with living death, make you an alcoholic, destroy your personality, neutralize your self-control, reduce you physically and mentally to a human vegetable. Three other bullets are aimed at your home, your job, and your integrity. They will make of you a problem drinker. Five of these fifteen bullets are deadly, and ten are blanks.

The liquor industry places this gun in your hand and says, "Play Russian roulette. Pull the trigger and take a chance! Only one bullet out of every three will get you." Moderate drinking is Russian roulette with a loaded pistol! As every third moderate drinker becomes either an alcoholic or a problem drinker, there is no psychological, physiological, medical, or scientific way to tell who that third victim may be. This is the *menace of moderation!*

The Big Lie continues: "But alcoholism is a *disease.* Therefore, if alcoholism is a disease, it dismisses the responsibility of the industry, the seller, and the partaker." Yes, alcoholism is a sickness—self-imposed, self-induced, and self-perpetuated. But this self-imposed sickness is not a disease like polio or cancer. There is no similarity. We are spending millions in research on polio and cancer to cure and to eradicate them. Physicians and the public have joined hands in a concerted effort to wipe out cancer and polio! Yet, on the other hand, we allow the liquor industry to spend hundreds of millions of dollars to persuade and encourage people to drink a poison that produces this so-called disease, alcoholism. Alcoholism *is* a curse. It *is* an evil. It *is* a sickness, a spiritual sickness and a moral failure that often becomes a psychological sickness. But it is not a disease.

The Big Lie is compounded: "Alcoholism is the result of personality maladjustments, neuroses, psychological weaknesses, and the tensions of the times. Don't blame the alcohol industry!" But Dr. William Lovejoy, outstanding Memphis pediatrician, has tersely reported the medical fact that "the prime cause of alcoholism is *alcohol*." There is only one place to put the blame for alcoholism—on the liquor industry. They produce the alcohol that produces the alcoholic!

The Big Lie is then simplified: "Alcoholism is only a problem of overindulgence. It is a sin to overindulge in anything. Intemperance in eating or drinking is the same." I know of people who have been arrested for driving while *drunk;* yet I have never known of a person arrested for driving while *fat!* There is no similarity in overindulgence in food and overindulgence in drink.

The Big Lie takes another approach: "The individual has the personal right to drink. It is a constitutional freedom, a great American heritage! We should not legislate so as to infringe upon this personal liberty." Yes, a citizen does have the personal right to drink in that he is a God-created, free moral agent. In this sense of the words "personal right," he is also free to commit adultery in the privacy of his bedroom, or to commit other private sins against his moral nature and the law of God. But when that sin, drinking or adultery, affects the rights of others, it becomes a social and legal concern of society.

When the exercise of a personal freedom infringes upon the rights and safety of others, society demands that these freedoms be relinquished. One bottle of beer so affects the nervous system of an automobile driver that it requires an extra six feet for a quick stop. If my child is in that six-foot death zone, the driver's so-called "freedom to drink just one bottle of beer" infringes upon *my liberty.* The driver should be deprived the right to drink even that one bottle.

The doctor has no right to drink and then stand over a patient with a scalpel in his hand. A pilot has no right to drink and fly a commercial airplane. Because of these social involvements of even moderate drinking, the personal right to drink should be denied by law to all members of an organized society, just as the law denies me the right to moderately steal or violate the traffic safety laws with moderation.

The Big Lie makes rebuttal: "But prohibition failed. Remember the gangsterism, the speak-easies, the lawlessness, the corruption?" Yet they do not tell you that in the first fifteen years after repeal the per capita consumption of liquor increased by fifteen times! If prohibition was a failure, repeal has been an even greater failure.

The Big Lie then pleads: "Give us time. Legalized liquor is the only answer. Look at France and Italy where liquor has long been legalized; you never see a drunk on the street!" Never has the truth been more distorted. France leads the world in alcoholics! Italy is second![1]

The Tragic Toll

As we have been sold the Big Lie of the liquor industry, our nation has paid a tragic physical and moral toll for giving unrestricted license to the beverage alcohol industry to operate legally and for giving the individual citizen unrestrained freedom to drink with "moderation," supervised only by his own self-discipline and discretion. The dismal heritage of moderate drinking and legalized liquor is staggering. The human carnage dumped on the ash heap of time by the liquor industry exceeds the combined devastation wrought by white slavery, the narcotic traffic, and even war!

A half-million husbands, sons, and sweethearts lost their lives defending our country in the two World Wars and Korea. If we were to stand in silent tribute watching a parade of these phantom dead march by, four abreast, forty inches apart, at three miles an hour, we would view a procession eighty-seven miles long. Add those wounded in these wars, and the column would be 147 miles long. It would require three days and nights for these heroes of the past to march by.

But imagine an even more tragic sight than this devastation of war. As Duke K. McCall said in an address, watch the army of America's "walking dead" stagger by—five million alcoholics who have been reduced to human vegetables, minds gone, wills wrecked, confirmed alcoholics, the living dead. Stand and watch them march by, day and night, in a line 869 miles long. Add to this column the three and a half million problem drinkers, making a total of eight and a half million problem drinkers, and you must stand for twenty-one heartbreaking days and nights to watch this parade of human derelicts. Every one of these alcoholics started drinking in moderation!

But the tragic toll in wrecked lives goes beyond eight and a half million alcoholics and problem drinkers. Alcoholism has been called America's *greatest unsolved health problem* by Dr. M. K. Callison of Memphis, Tennessee, specialist in internal medicine. Last year, acute alcoholism killed 15,000 people. It is the number four killer, with heart disease, first; cancer, second; and tuberculosis, third. Add the other deaths triggered by alcohol and it becomes the number one killer.[2]

In *The Scientific Monthly,* Dr. Raymond Pearl states that for every one hundred deaths of nondrinkers between thirty and sixty years of age, 152 hard drinkers die. There are nine times as many alcoholics as there are persons suffering from cancer, twenty times as many alcoholics as persons suffering from tuberculosis, and 268 times as many alcoholics as persons afflicted with polio before the Salk vaccine![3]

The drinking of beverage alcohol is also a primary social factor in our rising divorce rate and the disintegration of the American family. In Memphis, Tennessee, 25 per cent of the court divorces come from the single cause of alcoholism.[4] A Miami jurist Judge Cecil Curdy testified that if the true facts were always known, alcoholism would be the major cause in 90 per cent of the divorce cases.[5] J. Edgar Hoover adds that "the single factor in the rapid increase of juvenile delinquency and crime among youth is the drinking habit of youth or their parents, or both."[6]

It was reported in a Christian Life Conference meeting at Ridgecrest, North Carolina, that 83 per cent of the admissions to Baptist children homes in the last few years have not been orphans, but children from homes broken by alcohol. We must add to the rising heap of human carnage destroyed by beverage alcohol these millions of children whose lives have been blighted, happiness dimmed, and personalities warped by alcoholic parents and broken homes.

Yet the tragic toll of beverage alcohol is still greater. *Family Weekly* magazine, in an article "Drunken Drivers Are Getting Away with Murder," stated that last year 15,000 people were killed in automobile accidents involving a drunken driver and 800,000 others were injured or maimed.[7] This means that one of every eight families within the next two years will have one or more members of the family killed or maimed in an accident involving a drunken driver.

Or look at the cost in dollars! The University of Illinois recently published the results of a survey revealing that we are paying $125 million more in automobile insurance every year because of drunken drivers and their accidents. Dr. Marvin Brock of the American Medical Association has said that alcoholism is costing American industry and its workers a billion dollars a year in lost time and wages.[8]

Add to that the cost of crime induced by alcohol. The Metropolitan Life Insurance Company made a survey of 215 murders and found that in more than 50 per cent of the cases, either the victim or the slayer, or both, were drinking, or drunk, when the crime was committed.[9] Consider alcohol's contribution to other facets of the crime problem. The *Saturday Evening Post,* in a series of articles entitled "The Shame of America," reported that the great majority of girls who bore illegimate children were drunk at the time of their becoming pregnant. Professor A. G. Toynbee, the eminent British historian, in his book *Civilization on Trial,* sums up the toll we are paying by saying, "Alcohol is one of the chief agents in the disintegration of western civlization."

Alcoholism, the number one social and moral problem of our country, is the dismal heritage of moderate drinking. This problem is growing in complexity and proportion every day. There is a steady increase in the consumption of beverage alcohol, the number of "moderate" drinkers, and a corresponding rise in alcoholism and the attendant evils. Today, there are more liquor outlets in the United States than schools and churches combined. The Gallup poll of May 11, 1960, revealed a continuing upward trend in the drinking pattern of American adults. Sixty-two per cent of American adults now drink. This is a sharp increase of 7 per cent since 1958. Drinking is up in two notable areas: women and young adults. Seven out of every ten young adults drink. Already at a crisis level, the alcohol problem is increasing!

The Answer

What is the answer to this problem? A stepped-up salvage program for the eight and a half million alcoholics and hard drinkers is certainly needed. Alcoholics Anonymous is making the greatest contribution in this field. But they have reached less than 120,000 of these eight and a half million. Private and public clinics throughout the country do a notable job of salvaging alcoholics through medical treatment. But vitamin therapy, psychotherapy, and the drug disulfiram have helped less than 50,000 of the eight and a half million. For the alcoholic's sake, we need to do all possible to salvage and reclaim him, even though the results are negligible. But the Christian pulpit and the New Testament church cannot be content with a salvage operation, regardless of how extensive or successful it might be. We must also engage in a program of all-out prevention if we are to come to grips with this problem and make any substantial gains toward its solution.

Imagine for the moment a broad, level plateau. Imagine the edge of the plateau to be a precipice plunging downward a hundred feet to the valley below. Along this edge we have built a subdivision of new homes. As we move our families into our homes, with the backyards opening onto the dangerous precipice, we explain to our children the hazards of playing too close to the edge. One day a baby crawls to the precipice and plunges over to sudden death. In a back-yard football game, a player carelessly chases the ball near the edge. He, too, goes to an untimely death over the cliff. A teen-age couple, strolling in the moonlight, stumbles over the precipice in the darkness. One is killed and the other crippled for life.

Finally, a community assembly is called to study the problem. It is discovered that every family in the community is losing one child out of three over the cliff, so the parents make a great decision. They build a clinic at the bottom of the cliff, put an intern on duty, and station an ambulance at the base of the cliff. Then, whenever a child plunges over the precipice, the intern can rush to the child in the ambulance. If the child is not killed, the intern can patch up the broken body and, perhaps, save a life.

The parents are excited with the great possibilities of such a plan, for it is believed that they can save one out of every fifty or seventy-five children. They say that the beauty of this plan is that it does not restrict the freedom of the children to romp and play. To restrain or limit the area of their play would be a violation of their freedom. So the plan is to teach the children to *play moderately,* and educate them concerning the dangers of the cliff that borders on the yard where they play. And, though one out of every three children eventually will be lost over the cliff, the salvage program is set up at the base of the cliff to minister to those that survive.

That is the approach of the liquor industry. This has been the approach of too many loose-thinking Christians! Drink in moderation, and solve the alcohol problem with a bigger salvage program, a bigger hospital, more interns, and more ambulances to pick up those who plunge over the cliff.

I ask you, in the name of common sense, is this the solution? Of course, we would not discard the ambulance, tear down the hospital, or dismiss the intern. Of course, we would do all possible to salvage the unfortunates who fall over the cliff. *But the solution is to build a fence at the top of the cliff.* Build a fence so high and so strong that a child cannot get over it. True, occasionally a strong-willed child may in rebellion and disobedience climb over the fence in the dark of the night and plunge to destruction. Maintain the salvage station for such a wilful one. But build a fence to keep back the innocent, the careless, the thoughtless, and the immature.

The only answer to the alcohol problem is some fence building! I am interested in solutions, not just salvage. I am interested in the Christian church building some fences.

First, let us build some *personal fences*. Let us say, "As for me and my household, we will be total abstainers." We will not drink liquor, serve liquor, or possess liquor in our household. I want a big strong fence at the edge of the cliff in my home that my children may know that liquor has no place in my household.

Then, we need to build some *social fences*. Too long have we been manuevered into silence by the ridicule of the liquor industry. We have been caricatured as blue-nosed prohibitionists and cowed into timidity when we should have stood up and been counted!

I commend those who have positionized themselves as total abstainers in their clubs. I commend the officers who arranged a college alumni meeting that I attended recently. I was assured that cocktails would not be served before the dinner meeting. Two hundred people stood around in informal conversation before dinner drinking grape juice and having a wonderful time. Intelligent people do not need a cocktail to loosen up the conversation. You can have warm fellowship without a sloppy drunk hanging on your neck half the evening. Yes, it is high time for us as Christians to build some fences in our social circles and in our clubs.

We should continue building a stronger *educational fence*. In our Sunday schools and in our public schools we must continue to educate and inform young people and adults concerning the menace of moderation and the attendant evils of alcohol. We must give the facts and the truth to show up the Big Lie of the liquor industry.

Finally, I am for building strong *legal fences*. I believe we should build the legal fences so high and so strong as to make it very difficult for a person to climb over. I do not believe in putting liquor in drugstores, in grocery stores, and in an open front on Main Street. I believe in putting up such high legal fences that a person who wishes to drink must sneak out in the dark, go a long way, and climb high to find a bottle of whiskey.

Yes, I am a prohibitionist. I believe in prohibiting by law all criminal activity that endangers the life, health, and property of others. Beverage alcohol stands condemned as a criminal before every bar of justice human reason can erect and is also condemned before the bar of divine judgment. Yes, I believe in building some legal fences to outlaw beverage alcohol. I believe in citizens respecting those laws and I believe in expecting law-enforcement officers to enforce these laws rigidly.

However, we must also build some *moral* and *spiritual* *fences*. In the final analysis, this is a moral and spiritual problem that cannot be solved permanently by legal restrictions only. Liquor laws have not been effective because a large section of the public has not wanted them to be effective. Consequently, we have not had law enforcement because the public did not want law enforcement or was indifferent to it. We have had a weak conscience and a faltering conviction on this issue. This is a responsibility of the New Testament church to create a moral conscience that will result in courageous conviction and determined action.

Millions of years ago, giant dinosaurs ruled supreme throughout this continent. No creature on earth could match them in strength or size. Yet, eventually, these dreaded beasts died out, destroyed by a changing climate. In the final analysis, we will destroy the giant dragon of beverage alcohol only as we create the moral climate and spiritual environment in which legalized liquor will not be tolerated. This is the task of the New Testament church. This is the responsibility of every Christian. We may contribute to the creation of this new climate today by committing ourselves personally to total abstinence and pledging our total resources in all-out warfare to eradicate by legal and moral restraint the curse of beverage alcohol.

"Children, obey your parents in the Lord: for this is right. Honour thy father and mother; which is the first commandment with promise; That it may be well with thee, and thou mayest live long on the earth. And, ye fathers, provoke not your children to wrath: but bring them up in the nurture and admonition of the Lord" (Eph. 6:1-4).

6. Bad Boys and Delinquent Daughters

A PROMINENT citizen wrote, "The children now live in luxury. They have bad manners, contempt for authority . . . they no longer rise when elders enter the room. They contradict their parents, chatter before company, rattle dishes at the table, cross their legs and tyrannize over their teachers." This reads like the morning paper, but it was written 2,400 years ago by Socrates. Juvenile delinquency is not a new problem.

And juvenile delinquency is not a problem peculiar to Western society or to the United States. The May, 1960, issue of the State Department's publication *World Health* discusses the worldwide problem of troublesome teen-agers achieving notoriety in many countries. They are called *Teddy boys* in England, *stiliagi* in Russia, *achuligani* or *hooligans* in Poland and Czechoslovakia. They are the *black jackets* of France and the *leather jackets* of Sweden. They run in packs or gangs and commit the same type of offenses, criminal brutality, and vandalism as delinquents in the United States. They are antisocial and are in rebellion against the stable institutions of society. Two psychiatrists Dr. E. E. Krapf and Dr. Trevor Gibbens analyzed these delinquents as a peculiar product of our insecure society overshadowed with the threat of atomic annihilation and dominated by a fixation on sex.[1]

America's Number One Crime Problem

The fact that juvenile delinquency is neither a new problem nor peculiar to our own society does not relieve our concern since we recognize it as the number one crime problem of America. Senator Jacob Javits, Republican from New York, has proposed a five year $47 million crash program to combat this problem. He stated that youth crime is rising at an alarming rate and that unless an imaginative effort is made now to combat it, the crime picture will grow more bleak when these young offenders become hardened criminals. Included in his recommendations is a proposal for a national advisory council on juvenile delinquency. President Kennedy has since appointed this special council and has personally introduced this legislation to Congress.

Mr. J. Edgar Hoover, in the last FBI crime report, tells us that the crime rate is increasing five times faster than the population. The total crime bill last year was $22 billion, or an average of $128 for every citizen. A major crime is committed every twenty seconds. *The significant fact is that while adult crime is decreasing, youth crime is on the increase.* Half of the auto thefts are by persons under twenty-one, half of the burglaries are by persons under eighteen, and half of the crimes against property are by juveniles.

Parent's magazine reports that VD is on the rise again with a shocking increase among teen-agers. There was a 23 per cent increase in venereal disease in 1959 over the previous year, and an increase of 72 per cent in 1960 over 1959! More than one-half of the new cases reported fall in the 15-24 age group. The largest single age and sex group with venereal disease is the eighteen-year-old-girl bracket.[2]

This Week magazine reports an increase of 1000 per cent

in illegitimate births among high school students in thirteen Washington, D.C., public schools over a ten-year period. In New York during the first two months of the 1957 school year, 1,250 pregnant, unwed girls, fifteen years old or younger, were dismissed from the public schools. At the thirty-four Salvation Army homes for unmarried mothers throughout the country, the largest, single-age group admitted in recent years is the fifteen-year-old.[3]

Howard Whitman, writer on social issues, toured the country to survey the situation in the United States and Canada. In his syndicated articles on this problem, he cited examples of juvenile terrorism as follows: In Chatham, Ontario, scores of teen-agers were arrested after a forty-eight-hour binge of sex, liquor, and vandalism. In Dundalk, Maryland, teen-age vandals broke into a construction yard, set fire to a crane, poured sand into the compressor gas tanks, and slashed truck tires. At Fort Lauderdale, Florida, a wild, roving band of delinquents stole a city bus, smeared the city water tower with paint, threw coconuts through hotel windows, and smashed the windshields of parked cars.

Psychiatrists have thrown up their hands in despair. Police officers are puzzled and find no solution to the problem. Educators feel helpless in coping with the situation. A police captain said, "Something has happened to these kids in the last two or three years." A juvenile judge calls it a "disease of destruction." An educator calls it the three R's—raid, wreck, and ruin.

A Problem of the Home

This, then, is the issue we face. It is a problem that finds its cause in the home. And if it is ever solved, it must be solved *in the home.* The problem cannot be solved by the church, the school, or the public officials alone. Someone has calculated that a child has 108,000 waking hours in the period between infancy and maturity. Of this time, the average child will spend 1,000 hours in Sunday school and church, and 7,000 hours in the public schools. This accounts for 8,000 hours, leaving 100,000 hours to be spent by the child in the home under the supervision of the parents.

This problem is not limited to homes on the other side of the tracks. As Police Chief H. L. Park, of Los Angeles, stated, "Do not be led to believe that all of these delinquents come from the slum areas of our cities. A great number of them are from the better homes of the community."

Two Harvard researchers Sheldon and Eleanor Glueck studied thousands of cases of delinquency, painstakingly analyzing the home situations of the juveniles. Some of their discoveries can be summarized as follows:

Six out of ten delinquents had fathers or mothers who were excessive drinkers.

Three out of four delinquents had parents who exercised no oversight over their going or coming.

Three out of five delinquents lived in a family environment of constant wrangling and discord between the parents.

Seven out of ten delinquents came from families which had no group recreation in which all the family participated.

Four out of five delinquents said their parents never demonstrated or expressed affection for each other or toward the juvenile.

Few, if any, had religious training, and many of them were from broken homes.[4]

The inevitable conclusion is that delinquent parents are the chief producers of delinquent juveniles. Juveniles fail because their parents fail! *In the final analysis, the home is the chief breeding place of crime in our country.*

Ann Landers, in her syndicated column, recently reprinted twelve rules for raising delinquents. The original source is a bulletin issued by the Houston, Texas, Police Department.

1. Begin with infancy to give the child everything he wants. In this way he will grow up to believe the world owes him a living.
2. When he picks up bad words, laugh at him. This will make

him think he's cute. It will also encourage him to pick up "cuter" phrases that will blow off the top of your head.

3. Never give him any spiritual training. Wait until he is twenty-one; then let him "decide for himself."

4. Avoid the use of the word "wrong." It may develop a guilt complex. This will condition him to believe later, when he is arrested for stealing a car, that society is against him and he is being persecuted.

5. Pick up everything he leaves lying around—books, shoes, and clothing. Do everything for him so he will be experienced in throwing all responsibility onto others.

6. Let him read any printed matter he can get his hands on. Be careful that the silverware and glasses are sterilized, but let his mind feast on garbage.

7. Quarrel frequently in the presence of your children. In this way, they will not be too shocked when the home is broken up later.

8. Give a child all the spending money he wants. Never let him earn his own. Why should he have things as tough as YOU had them?

9. Satisfy his every craving for food, drink, and comfort. Denial may lead to frustration.

10. Take his part against neighbors, teachers, and policemen. They are all prejudiced against your child.

11. When he gets into real trouble apologize for yourself by saying, "I never could do anything with him."

12. Prepare for a life of grief. You will be apt to have it.

Below the surface humor here we see the tragic implication that some parents are living by these rules. They come to the minister every day with a heart broken by a son or a daughter gone bad and wonder why they failed as parents!

Rules for Parents

Here are some positive principles to guide you as a parent in dealing with your children.

1. Let your home be a house of love, filled with expression and acts of affection. Parents should express their love for each

other in front of the children, thus giving them a sense of security in the stability of the home. This also sets an ideal of marriage before the children, causing them to look forward to their own marriage. Parents should also express love toward the children themselves. If there is love in the home, the family can suffer many shocks and still be unmoved.

2. Spend time with your children. Spend time with each child—especially, father with son and mother with daughter. This causes a child to make the right identifications psychologically. Spend time as a family together in recreational activities. The kidnapper Carl Austin Hall, who figured in the Bobby Greenlease case, said, "Though my father was very wealthy, he never spent any time with me."

An envelope contained a father's Christmas gift to his young son. When the boy opened it, he read: "I promise to give you an hour of my time every day during the coming year." The little boy threw his arms around his daddy's neck and said, "This is the best Christmas present I ever got." Father, mother —cut loose from some of those club and social activities that are not really essential. Give more time to your most important responsibility, your child.

3. Be interested in your child's activities. Know who your children's friends are and where they go when they leave home. Have your children bring their friends into your home for social activities. In a trail-blazing, four-year, nation-wide survey, Harvard University psychologists analyzed 60,000 successful American families. This was a prime characteristic: The happy family gathers around itself a half-dozen other families of similar interests and ideals, and within this circle the children play together and stay together.[5]

4. Trust your children—but not their impulses! Have confidence in their integrity, but realize that they are still very immature in their moral judgments and in their self-disciplines. Keep your children away from difficult situations, and avoid exposing them to temptation. To refuse to allow your children to date at drive-in theaters, to make all the decisions in the

purchase of their clothing, or to take unchaperoned trips is not a refusal to trust them, but a recognition that they are not mature enough for you to trust their impulses.

5. Set definite limits and assign specific responsibilities to your children. Let your children know what they can and cannot do. This involves daily schedules for television, study, work, and play. The television in the American home is turned on an average of six hours a day, or forty-two hours a week. Last year 13,000 murders were committed on television. All kinds of acts of violence and crime were committed dramatically before millions of children.

No parents should allow the television to be on at all times without any regulation of the number and kind of programs. In our household, no television is allowed on school nights. On holidays and weekends, only a limited amount of television is permitted, and this rationed time is still subject to parental censorship. This also applies to movies.

The lead article in the March, 1961, issue of *Reader's Digest* deals with the problem of Hollywood's exploitation of sex. Ten major productions last year dealt with the subject of illicit sex. In five the heroine was a prostitute. There is no question but that juvenile delinquency has been increased by thoughtless parents who indiscriminately turn their children loose with television or send them to the movies "just to get them out from underfoot" to give the parents some leisure time. In addition to setting definite limits, give your children some chores and responsibilities around the house.

6. Discipline your children. The Bible says, "He that spareth his rod hateth his son: but he that loveth him chasteneth him" (Prov. 13:24). A New York magistrate declared that every Brooklyn home should have a woodshed, not necessarily for storing wood, either! My father never spanked his children on an empty stomach—he just turned us over and proceeded!

It would be surprising what a change some old-fashioned disciplining would make with some children. Have some broad principles, some fixed routines, and some firm rules established in the household. In advance, work out the penalties so that your children can know what to expect when they are disobedient. In this way, when you discipline a child physically or deny him privileges as punishment, the child knows his punishment is not just meted out in anger.

7. Keep the channels of communication open. Have an open-door policy. Talk things out with your children, and encourage them to talk their problems out with you.

8. Give your child a Christian example, some Christian ideals for living, and a regular routine of church participation. J. Edgar Hoover says that you should *take* your children to Sunday school. If Junior rebels, explain to him that everyone in the household goes to Sunday school and he is going too. Be firm as you would in having him bathe should he rebel against bathing! Keep your children in the church, and let them find their activities and their friends in church circles.

One of your greatest opportunities as a parent is to lead your boy or girl to Jesus Christ as Saviour. To prepare for this, give your child the example of a Christian daddy and a Christian mother. Less than 4 per cent of the juvenile delinquents come from church families. As you do this for your child, you can be sure that when he grows old he will not depart from it.

Rules for Teen-agers

And now a word to teen-agers. This is not a one-way street, young people! You have responsibilities as members of the family. Just as God expects your mother and father to be good parents, God makes some demands of you as a son or a daughter. Here are some rules for you.

Seek to understand your parents. Most teen-agers have middle-aged parents. Psychologists tell us that the two most crucial times in an individual's life are adolescence and middle age. When a person is going through either adolescence or middle age, great changes are taking place physically and psychologically. These two important lifelines cross at the same time in most families. The psychiatrist says that you teen-agers should have consideration for your parents as they are facing problems of adjustment just as you expect them to have consideration for you. One of my daughters excused her conduct by saying, "Daddy, I'm in one of those phases." She is, and I try to understand. But you should remember that daddies and mothers have phases, too. Try to understand why your mother is nervous, high strung, and irritable; or why your daddy seems unusually demanding or dictatorial at times.

Work hard at your job. Your father works hard and does a good job at bringing home a paycheck every week for you and the family. You are obligated to bring him home a good report card, with a C average or better, to show that you are working at your job as hard as he is at his.

Carry your share of work and responsibility around the house. If your father and mother provide you with food, clothing, and shelter, you are obligated to help with the chores. Remember you are not a star boarder but a part of the family. Express your appreciation in work and in words.

Forgive your parents and overlook their faults. Your mother may not be perfect. Your father may even stumble home drunk. But the fault and failure of your parents is no excuse for you to go haywire. In fact, you are obligated to forgive and overlook their weaknesses just as you expect them to forgive and overlook your faults.

Have you ever been disciplined at school, suspended, or even expelled? Have you ever wrecked the car, or been arrested for reckless driving? Have you ever been guilty of sponging off them or getting spending money from them when you ought to have earned it yourself? Remember how many times they overlook and forgive your failures and be willing to forgive them also. You are far from a perfect teen-ager, and you should not expect perfect parents.

Give your parents a Christian child. Give your heart and life to Jesus Christ and seek daily to live that life in a growing understanding of his will for it. This one gift, that of a Christian child, is the greatest gift that you can give your mother and father. With this gift you can repay them for every heartache you have ever caused them, every tear that has been shed and every sacrifice they have willingly made for you.

When Home Is Heaven

These are the simple rules for living together. If these rules prevailed in every family in our land, there would be no such problem as juvenile delinquency. Home would be heaven, and God would be accomplishing his purpose in the family.

A son had been drafted into military service. It was his last night at home. His mother and father waited for him to come in from the last date with his girl. Finally, they heard him come in and go to the kitchen. The father said, "Mother, I think I'll go downstairs and have a man-to-man talk with the boy, to give him some advice and counsel before he goes off to the army." Downstairs, he opened the kitchen door expecting to find the son raiding the refrigerator. Instead, he found him on his knees, praying. The father listened a moment, then quietly closed the door and went back upstairs. The mother asked, "Did you talk to him?" "No," he said, "I don't need to talk to him. Mother, our mission is fulfilled as parents. We have finished the job we started eighteen years ago when God sent the boy to us as a baby. It is all right for him to go to war now, for I have just seen him on his knees praying to God. He is relating his life to God completely, and we have finished the task God gave us as a mother and father." This is the job God has given to everyone of us as parents. God help us to see that task happily finished.

> "That they all may be one; as thou,
> Father, art in me, and I in thee, that they
> also may be one in us" (John 17:21).

7. Church Union and Denominationalism

NEVER before in world history has Christianity faced such a formidable array of enemies. Atheistic communism not only challenges the existence of the Christian community but threatens the survival of the very belief in God. The Soviet Union lost no time in capitalizing on Major Gagarin's feat in its campaign against religion. A recent broadcast in Ukrainian said the following: "Gagarin's exploit is of great atheistic importance. Religion has always contrasted earth and heaven. Now this concept has been shattered—heaven belongs to earth. Religion has been dealt a mortal blow by the human intellect and by the genius of the builders of Communism."[1]

In a recent television interview, Professor Arnold J. Toynbee said that, in his opinion, the religious concept of God could not survive the onslaught of communism unless all religions—Christianity, Mohammedanism, Buddhism, all who believe in a Supreme Being—unite in one great, worldwide, syncretistic faith. While we may not agree with Dr. Toynbee's proposal, we must admit that the challenge of communism demands from the Christian community a vital, effective witness.

Does this mean, however, a union of all churches into one great church to stand against communism? Pope John has already offered to Christendom the Roman Catholic Church as the worldwide union of Christians already established and organized to combat communism. The Catholic Church considers herself as the principal, if not the only, Christian deterrent to communism. It claims that there are only two ultimate positions in this struggle, Catholic or Communist. Though we may challenge the Roman Catholic claim, the question still faces us: Can communism be stopped by anything short of a union of all world Christians into one massive front, whether by the vehicle of the Roman Catholic ecclesiastical system or through some new ecumenical structure yet to be developed?

A second challenge to Christianity is the rapid growth of *paganism*. Thoughtful Christians must face the reality of the increasing unbelief of the world's population. The population explosion is in the pagan world! They are "outbirthing" us in a geometric progression. Christians are becoming a smaller percentage of the world's population with every tick of the clock. Evangelical Christians constitute 7 per cent of the world's population today; fifteen years from now they will be less than 5 per cent. We are frustrated by this overwhelming lostness and the seeming futility of our missionary endeavors. Can only a great, united, missionary movement sponsored by a single, united church save the situation?

The secularization of our own Christian society also threatens us. The challenge of materialism and a messianic hope in the white god of science confronts us!

In the face of such formidable foes, how can the church stand? We observe the success and effectiveness of high-powered organization in other areas of life. Government and business get bigger every day. Under the hypnotic influence of *organization*, many have concluded that the only answer to the problems facing Christendom is to be found in a superorganizational approach. They say that the fragmented influence of divided denominationalism cannot get the job done. They say that the multiplying of independent churches, duplicating the Christian message in the same community and the same geographical areas, hinders the Christian cause and dissipates money, personnel, and strength needed in Christianity's ultimate conflict. They say that Christianity can be saved only by a superorganizational approach to our problems.

The ecumenical approach as a solution to the problems facing Christianity is not new. The current campaign for Protestant union was launched a half-century ago in 1910 by the World Missionary Conference at Edinburgh. The textbook for this cause has been William Adam Brown's *Toward a United Church*. The World Council of Churches has been the cutting edge for the program. But in every decade, as churchmen faced this issue, they came to a hopeless impasse. The dilemma was this: If you are to have union, you must scrap your convictions. If you stand by your convictions, you cannot have union.

The Changing Internal Climate

But today, within the church, doctrinal divisions that separate evangelicals into denominations and Christendom into Catholic, Anglican, Greek Orthodox, and Protestant seem less significant to the average church member than ever before. This changed climate within the church has greatly favored the ecumenical cause. Sentiment among Protestants favoring one united Protestant church has climbed from 40 per cent in 1940 to 50 per cent in 1955. A larger number of undecided persons have lessened the number of those opposed to church union to 39 per cent.[2] A Catholic spokesman Father G. Baum, speaking in Toronto, is reported to have said that there is a changed theological atmosphere between Protestant communities and the Catholic Church. The new approach is based on the acknowledgment that all Christians, all baptized men believing in Christ, are brothers. He said, "We are not as far apart as we were in the past."[3]

Doctrinal Indifference

What has brought about this changed climate in which

divisive doctrines seem less important? Actually, what has happened is that doctrinal *difference* has been replaced by doctrinal *indifference*. A depth in doctrine creates differences. But a shallow faith is broadened to embrace anything for the sake of conformity. This popular approach to religion may be illustrated by the story of two Hollywood actresses discussing horoscopes. One said to the other, "I didn't know you believed in astrology." Her companion replied, "Oh, yes, I believe in *everything* a little bit."

This doctrinal indifference is the harvest of the neglect of Bible preaching and Bible teaching in the pulpit, resulting in Bible ignorance in the pew. Quite naturally, the average church member, without a biblical foundation for Christian faith and practice, views all churches as alike, even as in the dark all colors appear alike. Only light reveals the difference.

It was the open Bible and a turning to biblical faith that motivated the Protestant Reformation. Just as in the Dark Ages ignorance and coercion closed the Book to the common man and enslaved him in the tyranny and perversions of a heretical church, even so in this century the sly hand of indifference and neglect in pulpit and pew is closing the Bible to the average churchgoer.

With this indifference, also, has come the loss of a historical perspective and appreciation for a denominational heritage. This has produced a peculiar brand of theological education centered in the interdenominational theological school (ultra-liberal) on one extreme, and the nondenominational Bible college (actually *anti*denominational and hyperfundamental) on the other extreme. Although these schools seem to be antitheses, they are blood brothers in a common distaste for doctrine and an antipathy for denominationalism.

Another factor creating this doctrinal indifference is the increased popularity of the psychological application of the gospel. Too often, preaching and teaching has been "egocentric" instead of "theocentric." The emphasis in this interpretation of Christianity is not on what you *believe* or even what you *are,* but on how you *feel.* Christianity tells you how to overcome your inferiority complex, resolve all your anxieties, free yourself from all tension, and live confidently every day! A good Christian is a happy, cheerful extrovert, better able to enjoy all the blessings of our affluent society! Such phrases as "the man upstairs," "Somebody up there likes me," and "Why not try God?" (the theme of a Hollywood actress's testimony) picture to us a God who does favors for us in return for our favors done for him.

With this superficial interpretation of Christianity and lacking a biblically-based faith, many church members *do believe* that "one church is as good as another, and we all should get together as one great big family of Christians."

Roman-Protestant Union

Thus the ecumenical cause has been strengthened by external pressures mounting against the church and an increasingly favorable climate within the church. This has produced a flair of dramatic activity on the world scene that has caught the attention of all Christendom. In December, 1960, Dr. Geoffrey Fisher, retiring Archbishop of Canterbury and titular head of the Church of England, made a whirlwind, eleven-day tour of the church capitals of the world. He met with Patriarch Elishe Derderian, of the Armenian Church, in Jerusalem and Athenagoras I, the leading patriarch of the Orthodox Catholic Church, in Istanbul. These summital meetings were climaxed by a trip to Rome, where Dr. Fisher toppled a four-hundred-year-old tradition in a thirty-five minute conference with Pope John XXIII.

The last such conference was in 1530, when the Earl of Wiltshire led a delegation to Rome to discuss the problem of Henry VIII's divorce. Historians record that His Highness, in the traditional ritual, extended his toe to be kissed. But the visiting Englishmen refused to honor the proffered toe. However, the Earl's spaniel was uninhibited by ecclesiastical dignity. He seized the sacred toe in his teeth. There is some question as to whether it was the humiliating nip of the Earl's dog or Henry VIII's divorce that triggered the final break between the Roman Catholic Church and the Church of England. Be that as it may, for four centuries the door to the Vatican has been closed to official delegates from the Church of England.

Dr. Fisher's action comes as a natural expression of the Anglican church's interest in the ecumenical cause. Several years ago, I attended a service in London's Westminster Abbey. I heard a high churchman describe the Church of England as the "bridge church." He said it spanned the gulf between Catholicism and Protestantism, conserving the best of both traditions and destined of God to mediate a reconciliation that would reunite all of Christendom into one great catholic church.

As a result of this trip, Dr. Fisher is reported to have negotiated a future meeting between the Greek Orthodox patriarch Athenagoras, of the Eastern Church, and Pope John, of the Latin Church. If this meeting occurs, it will be the first such conference in more than a thousand years between leaders of the two churches. The schism which separated them occurred in A.D. 1054.

The fact that Pope John responded to Dr. Fisher's request for a conference to discuss closer fellowship is a reflection of the *new image* the Catholic Church is projecting under Pope John. He has publicly dedicated himself to effecting a reconciliation that "would bring back into the Roman fold all of those who had strayed." He established Monsignor Williebrands in the Vatican as the new Secretariat for Christian Unity, the first such office within the Roman Catholic hierarchy committed to work toward this ideal.

In the fall of 1960, the Vatican sent two official observers to the meeting of the central committee of the World Council of Churches. This move was acknowledged by all as a friendly gesture and interpreted by some as a formal recognition of the World Council by the Roman Church.

In spite of the dramatic activities of Pope John and Dr. Fisher, however, there is not a great deal of enthusiasm over the possibilities of a Protestant-Catholic merger. Dr. W. Stanford Reid said, "The only possible unity which can come between Protestants and Roman Catholics is the unity that Jonah had with the whale, namely that the Protestants should be swallowed."[4]

There is no evidence at all that the Roman Catholic Church is prepared to change its approach or modify claims of exclusiveness. Protestants see no signs that Catholics will give the Bible precedence over tradition on such matters as papal infallibility and the theological and liturgical status of the virgin Mary. These are insurmountable barriers. Father Raymond T. Bosler, editor of the *Criterion,* an archdiocesan weekly, is reported to have cautioned Catholic theologians working for church union to "be careful not to soft-pedal Catholic doctrine. We must come out quite frankly and say that this is where we stand."[5]

The Protestant Merger

Concurrent with these proposals for closer Catholic-Protestant ties has come a new call for Protestant union. Two facts should be noted in the current ecumenical movement, however. First, it is not a grass-roots surge. The dedicated disciples of church union are at the top levels of leadership. Second, the only common ground that has been suggested thus far has been bureaucratic and organizational rather than theological. No efforts, whatsoever, have been made to solve doctrinal differences. Most talk of union refers only to a unity in humanitarian benevolence and concern. These ecumenical proposals have not cut through to the real crux of the problem, that of doctrinal differences.

The most dramatic recent proposal was that of Dr. Eugene Carson Blake, a former president of the National Council of Churches. He has campaigned for a merger between the Presbyterian, Episcopalian, Methodist, and United Church of

Christ groups. The superchurch would be called the Reform and Catholic Church of the USA, knitting together 18,300,000 members, 42,000 churches, and 63,500 clergymen. The union would be primarily organizational, concerned with program and curriculum.

A suggested operational beachhead for this new united church was made at the last meeting of the National Council of Churches. It was proposed that the National Council itself be permitted to ordain clergymen, administer the sacraments, and accept individuals and denominations into its membership. It was proposed that all denominations immediately begin establishing new churches in new communities on a co-operative basis representing all denominations. Although this proposal was rejected, the trend of the National Council's interest was reflected in the fact that two-thirds of the program found itself devoted to a discussion of the cause of church union.

It is argued that the National Council of Churches is a *council* only, and that some groups have allowed a narrow sectarianism to keep them out of it. But though it claims an intent by name to be a council, it may be assumed that its leadership is committed to the ideal of an amalgamation of all denominations into one great, organic Protestant union. It would be a "new denomination to end denominationalism," as Dr. Blake has proposed. Actions, programs, and the statements of leadership all point the National Council of Churches toward this goal.

Bishop James A. Pike, of the Episcopal Church; Bishop John Wesley Lord, of the Methodist Church; and Dr. Fred Hoskins, of the United Church of Christ—all have spoken glowingly of the merger proposal as an answer to "fragmented witness" and "the scandal of our divided churches." Dr. Blake has stated that a divided church cannot proclaim convincingly a gospel of reconciling love and has called denominational barriers a sin. Dr. Pike, in a *Look* magazine article "The Church in Retreat," asserted that the church is losing its influence on society. He believes that the divided church, more and more sectarian in fact, is, therefore, less and less Christian in influence.

We would not question the right of these men to such personal opinions. However, we would challenge their authority to speak with finality in such a broad and sweeping indictment. Whereof do they speak of a "fragmented witness"? Is it the authority based on a particular ineffective pulpit with which they are familiar? Not everyone would be willing to acknowledge these men as authoritative spokesmen for all Protestant Christianity! Their statements are in striking contrast to the observation of perhaps the most eminent church historian of our day Dr. Kenneth Scott Latourette, emeritus professor of church history at Yale University. Dr. Latourette is reported to have said that *the present age is Christianity's best*. "Christianity is more widely spread than any other religion has ever been, the churches are more deeply rooted among more people than at any previous time, and the influence of Christ is spreading outside the Christian community." He credited Western Christianity (this is Hoskins's "fragmented witness" and Blake's "sinful denominationalism") with giving birth to most of the revolutionary forces and that much of the revolution has had its beginning among Protestant people.[6] In his opinion, apparently, divided Protestantism has had a vitality not noticeable in the monolithic Christianity of Old World Catholicism.

Questionable Gains

Many are not willing to concede that the *lack of union* has destroyed the effective witness of certain pulpits, churches, or denominations in our society. And we are not willing to grant that organizational union will automatically increase the effective witness of the church in society. Organizational unity in the Roman Catholic Church is a fact and has been one for fifteen centuries. *But such unity has not produced a corresponding spiritual power.*

Union would be imperative if it could be shown that *two plus two equals five*. Union would be *questionable* if it could be shown that *two plus two equals four*. For changing churches and members from one pocket to another in the name of conformity is pointless. But when *two plus two equals three*—then union becomes an enemy of vital Christianity as real as if it were a cause launched from hell! Yet every historical experiment in church union has resulted in the building of a church structure that has driven out the operation of the Spirit, has stifled New Testament truth, substituted tradition for biblical authority, and produced a spiritual sterility.

The Lesson of History

It is at this point that the ecumenical cause finds itself without defense. The ecumenical ideal of one united Church was achieved in the fourth century. For all practical purposes there was one Church in western Europe for twelve centuries to follow. Though there were dissenters and independent groups in all ages, the solidarity of this one Church was never effectively challenged until 1517. This Church perfected an ecclesiastical organization and a program and curriculum worldwide in scope. This powerful Church was a dominant factor in society. All areas of life felt the pressure of its influence—government, the courts, science, and education. And with this one superchurch came the heresies and perversions that were the scandal of the Dark Ages and the blight of contemporary Catholicism.

Pyramided ecclesiastical power compounds corruption. Carlyle Marney said, "Earthly unity is always a matter of power, and power always corrupts. The unity of institutions is a corrupt unity." Power corrupts the mind and morals of the most saintly men. Some of the most notorious moral degenerates were popes who served as the spiritual head of the Roman Catholic Church!

Power also breeds intolerance. As it increases in power, an ecclesiastical organization tends to become totalitarian and intolerant of differences of opinion. Conscience is coerced and an essential doctrine of New Testament Christianity, the priesthood of every believer, is vitiated.

Again, ecclesiastical systems and structures tend to absorb the spirit. Institutional requirements seem to limit the eternal Spirit of God. Spirit seems to decline in direct proportion to the increase in power of the ecclesiastical structure.

Furthermore, we observe that a giant superchurch organization falls easy prey to state domination. Through the centuries, the unholy alliance between the Church and the state has secularized the purposes of the Church and tyrannized the minds and bodies of men. Such an alliance is impossible when there are many separate, autonomous, free churches.

Our answer to the advocates of organic church union is the question: Have you not learned the lesson of history? The ecumenical ideal has been tried, tested, weighed, and found wanting through twelve centuries of experimentation.

A Constructive Position

Yet we have not absolved our responsibility in this issue by simply opposing organic church union. One cannot allow separatism to become an exclusiveness. The denomination is not the kingdom. A relationship of brotherhood and a unity of spirit with all other redeemed children of God must be acknowledged. Denominationalists have a responsibility to join with others in facing up to problems common to all Christendom. But these problems can be met best *by the strength and vitality that come from autonomy, not union.*

For example, there are almost as many different types of Baptists as there are Protestant denominational families. Some of the lesser known groups have included "Two-Seed-in-the-Spirit Baptists" and "Forty-gallon Baptists." However, there are four principal groups of Baptists in the United States making up twenty million members: Southern, American, and two National (Negro) conventions. They constitute the largest numerical body of non-Catholics in the United States.

Baptists have shied away from attempts to achieve organic union between any of their major bodies. Within these bodies, or conventions, are 75,000 independent and autonomous churches. This separatism and autonomy in some measure has been their strength. The rugged individualism of local, autonomous groups has compelled them to stand or fall on the basis of their spiritual vitality and to forge ahead to success or perish. Yet in all this freedom and autonomy, Baptists have demonstrated a marked ability to work together in co-operative efforts without a hierarchy. It is this principle of co-operative effort and unity of purpose and spirit without organic organizational unity that exemplifies the basis of their proposed relationship with all other denominations in Christendom.

Denominationalists should ever seek to find the good in other denominations and cultivate a common ground between them. They should respect the convictions of others. Honest differences exist. But in an atmosphere of honesty and freedom, they must find the areas of agreement and cultivate them. Conceive of the historical principles and doctrines of each denomination as represented by a circle. Certain parts of these circles will overlap with others, where the common ground is the same, as they converge on one another. These overlapping areas provide the basis for sympathetic understanding and co-operative effort. Our democratic form of government and our Western culture are based on this freedom and variety of individualism. And individualism overlaps into areas of corporate agreement and unity to give us a national and cultural solidarity.

At the *local level*, individual churches should develop many areas and enterprises for co-operation. There are moral and social issues on which local congregations of different denominations can unite and make an impact upon society.

At the *national level*, we should also cultivate areas of co-operation between all evangelicals. The essence of these conferences and co-operative enterprises should be *co-operational*, and not *corporational*. Dr. Ryland Knight, at the Southern

Baptist Convention meeting in Baltimore, Maryland, in 1940, presented a constructive position: "While we are fundamentally opposed to any steps toward organic union, we are convinced that the basic spirit of unity of all believers should have a channel through which to give united expression to the mind and message of Christ in the world."[7] This must have our earnest consideration.

We must ever seek out such channels and find a place of responsible service through them. For example, Southern Baptists have participated for many years with representation on the Uniform Lesson Committee of the Council of Religious Education. In the Foreign Mission Conference of North America we joined with other denominations in allocating areas of the world in which to work. Even now, seven major, independent, national Baptist bodies are engaged in a nation-wide, co-operative, six-year Jubilee Advance Program. This continent-wide crusade encompasses a co-operatively planned program in the field of evangelism, church extension, home and foreign missions, stewardships, and Bible study. In this enterprise, a unity of purpose has been accomplished without surrendering autonomy or conviction and without proposing a lateral unity.

The Unity of Christ

We believe that when Jesus prayed, in John 17:21, "that they all might be one," he was speaking of a unity of spirit centered in him. He spoke of a unity in a vertical line. Jesus was not praying for a horizontal, organizational unity of all believers into an ecclesiastical structure.

Let us meet the issues of the day, as vital Christianity has always done, by keeping our emphasis upon the spiritual nature of our faith and upon outward forms and organization only as they fitly belong to such a religion. Let us press through the maze of divided Christendom out into the open spaces of a *unity of spirit* and co-operation whereby the people of Christ can stand together without sacrificing conviction,

"Render therefore unto Caesar the things that are Caesar's; and unto God the things that are God's" (Matt. 22:21).

8. A Free Church in a Free State

O N September 12, 1960, campaigning Jack Kennedy said in Houston, Texas, "I believe in an America where the separation of the church and the state is absolute . . . where no Catholic prelate would tell the President how to act . . . where no church or church school is granted any public funds or political preference."[1] Immediately after inauguration, President Kennedy introduced a Federal Aid to Education program consistent with campaign commitments. Private and parochial schools were not included.

At once, the President's naive dream of freedom from religious pressure was shattered. Prelates of his own Church not only challenged his position, but in a block-busting campaign demanded that the President include Federal aid to Catholic schools in the proposed bill. They threatened to use the organized opposition of the Roman Catholic Church to wreck the program of Federal aid to education if their sectarian requests were not granted.

Cardinal Francis Spellman, archbishop of the New York Roman Catholic archdiocese, led the blistering attack charging discrimination against Catholic parents and pupils. Bishop Lawrence J. Shehan and Cardinal McIntyre joined in the campaign. The demands of the Catholic hierarchy were made clear: "Cut us in, or the baby dies!" Such pressure tactics used by the hierarchy without regard for Constitutional principle, national policy, or majority interests violates the American ideal of a free state and a free church, each autonomous in separate spheres.

We believe that when the church attempts to control the state by manipulating its membership as a power bloc in politics to gain sectarian advantage and privilege, that church has prostituted its spiritual character and abandoned its divine mission. The Bishop's threat to use the power of the Catholic Church to wreck the program unless they were "cut a piece of the Federal pie" is nothing less than ecclesiastical blackmail. Justifiable resentment has been expressed by Protestants and freedom-loving Catholic laymen alike.

As this dramatic challenge has been made by the Roman Catholic hierarchy to one of their favorite sons, we join with other Americans in our personal expectation that President Kennedy will keep faith with his stated convictions and adhere to the further pledge, also made at the Houston Ministers' Conference, "I will make my decisions . . . without regard to outside religious pressures or dictates." Kennedy further stated that he would resign his office rather than compromise this principle.[2]

Though Kennedy's future position on the church-state issue is uncertain, this clear prediction and forthright statement can be made: *We are facing the greatest challenge to Constitutional liberty and the ideal of religious freedom that the American Republic has ever known!* This is not a mere Protestant-Catholic squabble of the moment. Neither is this a purely religious issue. President Kennedy himself has stated that tax support of church institutions is contrary to the Constitution of the United States.[3] Regardless of the outcome of a particular piece of legislation providing Federal aid to parochial schools, the battle will continue unabated. The issue is that the Roman Catholic Church has declared war against the Constitution of the United States, the principle of the separation of the church and the State, and the First Amendment to the Constitution in particular. Because of this declaration of war we are engaged in a life-and-death struggle for religious freedom. As the battle lines are being drawn, the Roman hierarchy has openly set forth their four objectives. They are stairsteps to total victory.

Step one is the destruction of the American public school system. The first objective of the Roman Catholic hierarchy is to dismember, displace, and ultimately destroy the public school system of America. We believe that free public education, a responsibility of the State, developed and supported as a function of the State for all citizens, is mandatory to a democracy. We believe that the free public school system has been a principal factor in the development and rise of a middle class in our country. We believe that a free public school system is a necessary bulwark for the preservation of democracy in a world plunging toward totalitarian communism.

But the Roman Catholic Church does not share in these beliefs. The Roman Church consistently asserts that education is not a proper function of the State but is the rightful province and responsibility of the Church. Its objective is to displace and supersede the public school system with a parochial school system operated by the Catholic Church and paid for by the State. Pope Pius XI on December 31, 1929, in a special encyclical, made this clear when he said, "The attendance of Catholic children in non-Catholic schools is forbidden and can only be tolerated at the discretion of the Bishops. It is the duty of the state to help the church maintain its religious schools by aid from public funds" (Canon Law 1374).

Every conceivable method of coercion is used to make attendance at parochial schools compulsory for all Catholic children. As a result, there are five and a half million pupils in 15,000 Catholic schools in the United States. This is one student for every seven enrolled in the public school system. A shocking practice designed by the Catholic Church to further coerce the choice of the Catholic graduate seeking admission to college was revealed by an article in the August,

1960, issue of *College Board Review,* official publication of the College Entrance Board. The article stated that the heads of some Roman Catholic secondary schools *refuse* to send recommendations or transcripts for Roman Catholic students attempting to enrol in non-Catholic colleges.

The *New York Post* on August 9, 1960, said that a recent survey of admission officers of New York colleges disclosed a pattern of obstruction in sending such items to non-Catholic colleges. The paper quotes Henry S. Coleman, admissions director at Columbia, as saying that Roman Catholic school officials frequently and purposely send out poor reports. "They grade them in the lowest possible category, usually in the bottom ten percent," he said. The priests undoubtedly hope that the students, refused entrance into non-Catholic colleges, will settle for a college where subjects are taught as dictated by Church leaders.

The Catholic Church has now built a huge educational empire in competition with our public school system. In many places—such as Dallas, Louisville, and New Orleans—they have been able to provide better buildings and curriculum than the public schools (especially at the high school level). Many non-Catholic pupils are attracted to these private schools.

This sweet taste of success has now caused the Roman Catholic hierarchy to press for victory in shifting the financial responsibility of this huge, private, competitive, institutional empire onto the shoulders of the American taxpayer, so it can be still more effective in putting the public school system out of business. In a five to four ruling, the Supreme Court already has declared that public tax money may go for the transportation of pupils to parochial schools.[4] Note, in passing, the significance of one judge's decision. It was a five to four ruling!

In California, under Catholic governor Pat Brown, five Supreme Court justices were appointed. All five were Catholics! How will the Constitution be interpreted in the future as a Catholic governor or president packs the court with judges slanted toward a Catholic interpretation of law? Yesterday, the issue was tax money for the transportation of pupils to parochial schools. Today, it is Federal money for buildings and tuition for students in Church schools. Tomorrow, it well may be public funds for salaries, administrative costs, and total support. Cardinal Spellman said that not to do so is to "discriminate against Catholics."

The claim of discrimination is ridiculous. For example, a community needs roads. This is a public responsibility. The Government builds and maintains public roads with tax money. I pay my share of road cost and maintenance through taxes whether I drive a car on these roads or not. I may even choose to build a private road on my private property for my private travel. But this I must do at my own expense!

In the same way, a community needs schools. It is the responsibility of Government to provide and make available public school education for all. All citizens—the family man, the couple without children, and even the bachelor—share financially in this responsibility.   A devotee of the private school system has the option to build a private school and send his own child to the private school at his own expense. But the fact that a citizen travels a private road, or sends his children to a private school, does not exempt that citizen from paying taxes for the support of public roads and public schools. Nor does it entitle him to a refund of his tax money to maintain his private road or his private school. In spite of the lack of logic and principle in their claims, the Roman hierarchy continues an all-out drive to get public tax money for parochial schools.

While building up a private parochial school system, the Catholic Church is also in a concerted drive to capture control of local public schools by gaining a majority control on local school boards. The "captive" public school is then converted into a parochial school. A typical example of this strategy in practice is the Johnsburg, Illinois, case, one of twenty-nine similar cases in the state.[5] There, Catholic candidates won positions on the school board until, by a majority vote, they fired the competent and qualified public school teachers and replaced them with poorly qualified, garbed nuns, many even lacking proper certification. They replaced the textbooks with Catholic texts, and introduced Catholic doctrinal teachings and Catholic symbols into the classroom. The schools were restored to public operation and freed from Catholic control only after a lengthy court fight.

This same strategy has been repeated in Kansas where, at the last count, 152 garbed nuns were teaching in the public schools.[6] Today, there are hundreds of "captured schools" in at least twenty-two states, according to the POAU (Protestants and Other Americans for the separation of Church and State). Today, 120,000 garbed nuns teach in the public and private schoolrooms in America. Foy Valentine, of the Christian Life Commission of the Southern Baptist Convention, estimated that over $100 million of school tax money in the past ten years has gone directly to the Catholic Church through salaries paid to garbed nuns teaching in the public school systems.[7] (Nuns take vows of poverty. They teach for board and keep only and sign all salary checks over to the Catholic Church.) In Indiana, in the past two years alone, an estimated $2 million of public school funds has flowed into the coffers of the Catholic Church through this same channel.[8]

Often, if the lack of a majority, or public pressure, or legal restraint prevents the capture of a local public school, Catholic school board members then become obstructionists, retarding the development of the public system to keep it inferior, inadequately staffed, ill-equipped, and housed in dilapidated buildings. The appeal is to "keep down taxes," but the effect is to create a gap between a poorly-financed public school system and a well-financed parochial school system.

Thus the battle is waged with a two-edged sword, one edge the building up of a private, competitive school system, and the other edge wrecking or absorbing the existing public school system. The length to which the Roman Catholic Church will go to sabotage the public school system is illustrated by a news release from Canada of April, 1961, reporting that the Church *threatened to deny school board members absolution for their sins if they compelled Catholic citizens to pay taxes for public schools.* The full account of this ruthless spiritual tyranny reads:

Msgr. J. N. Gelineau, vicar general of the Ottaway Roman Catholic archdiocese, warned Catholic public school trustees in Ontario Province that the church may deny them absolution if they insist on Catholics paying taxes to public school boards instead of to separate [Catholic] boards.

He declared: "It is not permissible for Catholics to pay school taxes to benefit public schools. Persons going against Directive 268 of the archdiocese will not be worthy of absolution."[9]

We need only to look at Spain or Colombia to see what happens when this Catholic ideal of education, conducted and controlled by the Church and financed by the state, is achieved. In Colombia, recently, I witnessed the discrimination leveled against the children of non-Catholics by a Catholic-controlled school system. I met children from evangelical families who had been threatened and ridiculed in the school room. They were finally expelled from school simply because their parents attended a non-Catholic church and because these parents refused to yield to pressure to quit their church. Consequently, they are compelled to operate a school with every mission or chapel for the children of their own church members in Colombia. They are denied the right to send their children to the Catholic-controlled public schools simply because they have exercised freedom of conscience in religious matters and have chosen a belief and a church other than Catholic.

This same pattern of persecution has long prevailed in Spain. In a visit to mission work there, where there were once seven thousand children in evangelical schools, I found that the government has now closed these schools and made it illegal for evangelical churches to operate schools. Today, in

Spain, the Catholic Church supervises all the functions of education, operates all schools, and uses the classroom to indoctrinate pupils in Catholic belief.

Further brainwashing and thought control is accomplished by making it illegal for evangelicals to publish a paper or magazine, print literature, publish or import Bibles, or to answer Catholic charges against them on the radio or in the press. Evangelicals cannot identify their buildings with signs, visit, or propagate their doctrine in any way. If the Roman Catholic hierarchy can destroy the American public school system and take over as a Church function the responsibility for education, we can expect similar attempts at thought control in our society.

The second step of the Roman Catholic hierarchy is to batter down the wall of separation between the church and the State. This wall is established by the First Amendment to the Constitution. The drive for public funds for parochial schools is only a minor skirmish in this larger campaign. The campaign is also pressed on other fronts. Tax money for other Catholic institutions is already an accomplished fact. Under the Hill-Burton Act, 92 per cent of the money allocated to denominational hospitals went to the Catholic welfare empire composed of 1,500 hospitals.

Recently, Bishop Fulton J. Sheen, in testimony before a Congressional committee, proposed that all foreign aid be channeled through the Catholic Church. The Bishop said that in so doing we would give a spiritual meaning and significance to American money spent abroad.[10] A proposal was also made that all surplus government property abroad be turned over to Catholic organizations and missionaries for Church use on foreign fields. Although no legislation as yet has set forth such a policy of funneling aid through the Catholic Church, nevertheless, much of our foreign aid has gone by this route!

Dr. Breeden, medical missionary with the Baptist Hospital in Barranquilla, Colombia, confirms this fact. When I visited the mission work there, he told me that it is practically impossible in Colombia for a Protestant institution or a Protestant family to receive any assistance, medical supplies, foodstuffs, or clothing from the United States through State Department or Red Cross channels.   The Catholic Church controls the disbursement of such aid.

Let us see the issue clearly. A few million dollars channeled to parochial schools for student aid or in building loans is not the single objective of the Roman Catholic hierarchy. This is only one prong of a gigantic thrust to breach the wall of separation between church and State and repeal the First Amendment to the Constitution. Father Patrick O'Brien is quoted as setting forth this bold intention of the Catholic Church: "If necessary we will change, amend, or blot out the present Constitution so that the President may enforce . . . our . . . program . . . as laid down by our saintly Pope and Holy Mother Church."[11]   This is a restatement of the Catholic Bishops joint declaration of November 21, 1948, calling for the faithful to work patiently and persistently for the destruction of the wall separating the church and the State. This is the clearly defined, openly stated, published objective of the Roman Catholic hierarchy.

There follows the third objective of the Roman Catholic hierarchy: curtailment of religious freedom for all non-Catholics. To us, this means the loss of religious liberty. To us, this means the destruction of the free atmosphere that we enjoy to worship God according to the dictates of our own conscience and not according to the dictates of a state Church.   This freedom is a distinctive contribution of America to the philosophy of government. This treasured religious liberty is possessed by citizens in no more than a half-dozen other nations in the world.

You say, "This is too much! Catholic denial of full religious freedom to non-Catholics may occur in Europe and Latin America, but it could never happen here." But it already does happen here wherever Catholic pressure can be mounted, political or otherwise, in a community. The news publication

Church and State reported that a pastor, Robert P. Dugans, Jr., was barred from radio station WWNH because he gave a Protestant interpretation over the air of Matthew 16:13-30. The Roman Catholic Church claims to be founded on the person of Peter while evangelicals say that Christ founded the church on Peter's confession. Pastor Dugans supposed he was preaching in a free country, but he found that a radio station controlled by Catholic interest in a Catholic community barred him from the air. This did not happen in Spain during the Inquisition; this happened in Rochester, New York, in 1960!

In Ohio, three preachers were arrested for preaching on the sidewalk across the street from the courthouse.[12] This did not happen in colonial America two centuries ago. It happened in 1961 in Cleveland!

A church is denied a building permit without grounds. There is no recourse in the Catholic-dominated political atmosphere. This did not happen in Argentina where non-Catholics are barred from public office, but in Boston, Massachusetts!

A Catholic-dominated zoning board compels a church to turn off its neon sign on Sunday night, even though the church has been in that location for fifty years and the sign has been used for many years. This is not in Spain, where Protestants are forbidden to identify their house of worship with a sign, but in Chicago, Illinois!

Reverend Norman Pipe, of Canada, told of Baptist pastors in the province of Quebec who have been jailed, up to a total of two hundred days each, for preaching the gospel. They were arrested by Catholic officers and convicted by Catholic officials. This happened, not in Colombia where priest-led mobs have burned evangelical church buildings and stoned worshipers, but on the North American continent just beyond the borders of the United States.

This is the story today. What does the future hold? Will we be denied the right to print our hymnbooks tomorrow? That right is denied to us in Catholic Spain. Will we be denied the right to distribute the Bible publicly? That right is denied us in Catholic Colombia. I stood on the streets in Bogota, Colombia, handing out copies of the Gospel of John to children. The missionary informed me that I was violating the law and could be arrested and severely punished for committing the crime of publicly distributing religious literature, even though it was a portion of the Bible.

I fully realize the responsibility involved in making these statements. I charge that the Roman Catholic Church has the objective of curtailing and denying religious freedom to all non-Catholics. I cite these examples from my personal knowledge where these rights have already been infringed upon. But I also cite the clear-cut, openly published declaration of the Catholic Church on this matter. The Papal Encyclical entitled *Immortali Dei* of Pope Leo XIII, issued on November 1, 1885, clearly lays down the Catholic principle of religious liberty *for Catholics only.*

Father John A. Ryan, in the book *Catholic Principles of Politics,* published in 1940 and bearing the imprimatur of Cardinal Spellman, said: "Whenever that church [the Roman Catholic Church] secures a position of overwhelming majority in a nation, it has the right to expect the state to *impose restrictions on all non-Catholics in their religious teachings and propaganda, and deny them privileges extended to the Roman Catholic Church* [Italics mine]."[13]

This is the avowed, published, open, declared goal of the Catholic hierarchy for America. When this majority is gained in a ward, political district, city, county, state, or nation, the religious rights of non-Catholics will be curtailed and special privileges granted to the Roman Catholic Church. Do not say it cannot happen here as in Spain or Colombia. It is happening here, today!

The fourth objective of Roman Catholicism is a Catholic America. Thus the hierarchy's program for America is summed up in these four progressive steps. Step one is to eclipse and eventually replace the public school system with

Church-controlled schools supported by public tax funds. The second step is to breach the wall of separation between the church and the State by repeal of the First Amendment. The third step is to restrict the religious freedom and activities of non-Catholics, for as the Catholic Church has always declared, "Error has no rights." John A. Ryan clearly sets this forth in his book *Catholic Principles of Politics:* "The fact that the individual may in good faith think that his false religion is true gives no more right to propagate it. . . . How can error have rights?"[14] These three steps lead to the ultimate step, to make America Catholic.

We are staggered by the rapidity with which Catholics are moving toward this final objective. In 1790, there were 30,000 Catholics in the United States, one out of every 139 citizens. Forty years later, in 1830, the Catholic population had increased to one out of every 42. In the 1960 census, the Catholic population was one out of five. Today, one of every three church members is a Catholic. There are eighty million evangelicals and forty million Catholics in the United States. The eighty million evangelicals split and divide into more than two hundred denominations while the forty million Catholics are unified in a solid, monolithic, organizational and doctrinal structure.

The sheer size and power of this massive ecclesiastical institution frightens many Americans, especially as they realize the high degree of rigid discipline and control the Catholic Church exercises over all areas in the lives of its communicants. It has a hierarchy of 190 bishops and 31 archbishops, 6 of whom are cardinals. It is served by 54,000 priests and 165,000 nuns in the 17,000 parishes and 5,000 missions. Two hundred and forty national Catholic societies buttress this Church organization, of which 150 are action groups, organized and committed to control, pressure, and influence every sector of national life.

The political power of the Catholic action groups was demonstrated in the 1960 national election. In 1957, Catholic leaders of New England promised the politicians that they could deliver a solid Catholic vote in any national election. On November 8, 1960, they delivered this vote for Catholic candidate Kennedy. This happened in the land of Roger Williams, of the Puritans, of Finney and Moody, a land once a great evangelical stronghold.

As the thrust to make America Catholic gains momentum, the appeal is made: *Catholicism is the only defense against communism.* Bishop Fulton J. Sheen cleverly set two alternatives before us: We must take either "the road to Moscow or the road to Rome." We look at both roads as unsafe, however, for the end of each road is *slavery.* Some persons would speculate as to which is more oppressive, communist tyranny or Catholic tyranny. To say the least, the Russian Baptist church in communistic Moscow enjoys more religious freedom today than the Spanish Baptist church in Catholic Madrid.

The Answer

This, then, is the problem: a cumulative drive in four steps to make America Catholic. A powerfully organized hierarchy is moving us adroitly toward this objective. In the last ten years, Catholicism had a net gain of 44 per cent while all evangelicals had a net gain of 22 per cent.[15] Catholics are increasing twice as fast as evangelicals. If we are to be true to our commission and witness as New Testament Christians, we must meet this new challenge with a *message* and a *method* that will turn the tide.

Our Message

This is our message: a faith built on *truth,* not *tradition.* Jesus said, "Ye shall know the truth, and the truth shall make you free" (John 8:32). The pillars of our faith are fashioned from the two materials of *truth* and *freedom.*

The first pillar is *freedom of conscience.* The New Testament proclaims the priesthood of every believer, which gives to every man the right and responsibility to worship as his conscience dictates and to make his own moral and spiritual judgments, free from the dictates of ecclesiastic authority, creed, or tradition.

The second pillar is *freedom of grace*. The New Testament truth is "by grace are ye saved, through faith." Salvation is the free gift of God's grace—not to be doled out by any priestly class of men; not to be dispensed by any church which conceives itself as the sole custodian of salvation; not to be earned by good deeds; and not to be purchased with the coin of any realm.

The third pillar is *freedom of access to God*. We pray neither to, nor through, any earthly man or heavenly figure save Jesus Christ. He is our sole mediator, who is constantly beside the Father in our behalf.

The fourth pillar is *freedom of religion from authoritarian control*. We believe in religious liberty, not simply toleration, as the inherent right of every soul. We vigorously resist all efforts of any government, whether political or ecclesiastical or both, to dictate to the religious conscience of men, or to underwrite or establish a state church. To make this freedom an accomplished fact, we believe in the complete separation of the church and the state. Thus the state cannot grant special privilege to any church, and citizens are not compelled to give support in any manner to any church against their will.

Our opposition to the growing power of Catholicism is not one of sour grapes for their success or of negative vilification. It is an opposition born of sincere conflict as we bring to bear these basic New Testament truths and historic democratic principles on the doctrines and practices of Catholicism, and as we observe its consistent deviation and departure therefrom.

Our Method

As there is a basic conflict in message between evangelicalism and Catholicism, there is also a conflict in method. We believe that the New Testament method for evangelizing the world is to be by *persuasion* and not *coercion*. When the truth that is in Christ Jesus, and recorded for us in the divinely inspired Word of God, is brought to bear on an open mind by the power of preaching and persuasion, men are won to God, and his kingdom is established among men.

But whenever that truth is suppressed, as in the denial of the right to distribute religious literature; whenever the preacher is muzzled, by force or civil ordinance; whenever the mind is coerced, through thought control, and suppression of free discussion of all sides of an issue; whenever freedom of choice is denied the individual, as in infant baptism and sacramental salvation—we then believe that coercion has replaced persuasion. Such coercion is, in principle, the same as confession by torture as practiced during the long Spanish Inquisition. And such methods are absolutely repugnant to us who believe in the freedom and competency of the individual soul in matters religious and spiritual.

We believe in a free pulpit, and freedom to all faiths to proclaim their views, trusting that truth will win the minds of men by the power of free persuasion. In this, we have been Catholicism's best friend in providing this atmosphere of freedom in which the Catholic Church has enjoyed unprecedented liberty and success as a minority group to propagate and proclaim its faith. The ironic fact is that, having been the chief beneficiary of this climate of freedom as a minority group, the Roman Catholic hierarchy is now flexing its muscles in a threat to assert itself as a new majority power bloc in American life. As such, they are seeking to change completely the religious climate to one of coercion and tyranny over all non-Catholics, and preferential treatment for their own Church. This is the challenge that we now face.

This challenge must be met *openly*. We must speak up, and speak out, on these religious and political issues wherein we differ with the Catholic hierarchy. The right to free expression of opinion is essential in a democracy. We are not "bigots" to question, challenge, or refute the doctrines and practices of a religious or political group with which we differ. This is the essence of freedom of speech. The bigot is he who would muzzle, silence, abuse, or ridicule this free expression. Now is a time for ministers and laymen alike to speak their piece on these issues, regardless of the name calling and intolerant criticism that may follow.

This challenge must be met with *conviction*. Broad, loose conformity can never give the motivation and power to win the victory. We will never win this battle, and a battle it is, by lukewarm, insipid conformity and indifference. As Glenn L. Archer, Executive Secretary of POAU, said in a letter to me, "What if Winston Churchill had said, 'I think we ought to fight on the beaches; or at least this is my opinion. Some of the others may disagree with me. But if we can't fight there, perhaps we would like to fight in the mountains, unless there is somebody who objects.' The Battle for Britain would have been lost from the start!" Even so, as we waver and weaken in indecision, compromise, and loose conformity, we will lose this battle.

We must meet this challenge with *courage*. Silence is cowardice. But courageous conviction is the heritage granted to us by thousands in past generations who have waged and won this bloody battle for truth and freedom. There was Balthasar Hubmaier, who renounced the priesthood to become an Anabaptist. He was arrested, tortured, and on March 10, 1528, burned at the stake in the Vienna public square because he refused to recant the view that the Lord's Supper and believers' baptism were the only two true ordinances of the New Testament.

There was John Bunyan, a hundred years later, who was arrested in England for preaching without a license from the state church. He was imprisoned in Bedford jail for more than ten years for this offense. When offered his freedom for the promise to cease preaching, he answered, "I'll stay in this prison until moss grows on my eyebrows before I make such a promise."

There was Obadiah Holmes, one of forty-two Baptist

preachers arrested in Virginia in 1651 for preaching the gospel. After he was punished with thirty lashes of the horsewhip in a public beating administered by the sheriff, he said, "You have beaten me as with roses." This is our heritage, of bloodshed and lives poured out to give to us and to the world this unique, democratic form of government with full religious liberty, free from an authoritative state religion and ecclesiastical tyranny.

This is a great heritage! This is a great day to claim this heritage and proclaim this gospel delivered unto us by blood-stained hands. Today, there are eighty million uncommitted people in the United States. They are neither evangelical nor Catholic; not Baptist, Methodist, or Presbyterian. They live in a spiritual vacuum! They know no loyalty to any church or creed. They have had no soul-saving, life-redeeming experience in Jesus Christ. This is the vast army of eighty million people we call lost and unenlisted. These people will determine the destiny of America. Whoever wins these eighty million uncommitted souls will win America. We are in a life-and-death struggle to win them. We will win them to our way, or they will be won to another persuasion. They will not continue in a spiritual vacuum.

A general asked Alexander the Great, "To whom will go the kingdom after you are gone?" He answered, "The kingdom belongs to him who can take it." The future belongs to those who take it. If we sit in our comfortable churches, indifferent to the issues of the day and unresponsive to the lost and unenlisted people that surround us, we will have no one but ourselves to blame when, in some dark tomorrow, we find that we have lost the battle.

Napoleon said, "Conquest has made me what I am, and conquest must maintain me." Evangelism has made us what we are, and evangelism must maintain us. This is a great day for evangelism, for soul winning, for Bible study, for visitation, for the teaching and the preaching of the gospel! This is a great day to be a Sunday school teacher! The destiny of America will not be cast in some far-off, distant future. It is being determined now! The future of America is not being settled in a conference on the other side of the world, but it is being settled in the councils of Christian people in our church, and in our communities today. We will save the day for New Testament Christianity and for the American ideal of religious freedom only as we commit ourselves anew and afresh to the proclamation of the gospel and to reaching these eighty million uncommitted souls for Jesus Christ in an unprecedented program of outreach for the unreached!

"I am the way, the truth, and the life: no man cometh unto the Father, but by me" (John 14:6).

9. Religion Versus Christianity

HE said, "We're all strivin' for the same place. You go one way and I go another. But the way doesn't matter, just so long as we get there! If a man's got religion and he's sincere, he's got all he needs to live and die by."

In a Buddhist shrine in Honolulu, I heard a soft-spoken Oriental priestess express the same idea, but she was far more poetic: "Many pathways lead up the mountain. We believe that all who sincerely press on the upward way will eventually arrive at the mountaintop to view the same moonlight together." This, then, is the question: "Is one religion as good as another if it is sincerely believed and followed? Will any path, sincerely pursued, eventually lead us to God?"

The Profusion of Religion

Look for a moment at a few of the many pathways by which men have sought God.

Seven thousand years ago at Byblos on the eastern coast of the Mediterranean Sea, a very religious man died. He was buried in an earthen jar or urn. I saw him with knees drawn up under his chin, arms folded, head turned to the side in the exact prenatal position of an unborn babe. He died believing that from this earthy womb of clay he would be born again into a new life beyond the grave. This was his religion. He was sincere! He believed it, lived by it, and died by it!

Five thousand years ago in a pyramid tomb at the desert

edge of the River Nile, the body of Cheops, Child of the Sun, Ruler of the Universe, and Pharaoh of Egypt was laid to rest. His was a different pathway up the mountain. He believed that every day the sun was swallowed by the goddess of darkness to pass through her body at night and be born again with the sunrise. He believed that at death he, too, was swallowed by this black goddess, and that he would be born again with the sun to ride at the side of his father beyond the gates of the stars. In the sands beside the great pyramid, you may see the solar boat, thirty feet long, fashioned from the cedars of Lebanon to carry Cheops and all his court in an eternal orbit across the heavens. This was his religion. He believed it, lived by it, and died by it!

Four thousand years ago, when Abraham journeyed from Ur of Chaldees into the land of the Canaanites that lay between the Lebanons and the Anti-Lebanons, he found another very religious people. Their upward path was by the way of Astarte, goddess of love and fertility. Stand with me amid the magnificent columned ruins at Baalbek in Syria where Abraham must have stood. See the very temple where thousands of priestesses served as holy prostitutes in indescribable orgies of immoral debauchery and paganistic worship. This was their religion. They believed it, lived by it, and died by it!

Two thousand years ago, pious Jewish pilgrims by the thousands made their way to Jerusalem into the temple on Mount Moriah. There the high altar was a rock, believed to be the very rock on which Abraham offered his son, Isaac. See this rock, coursed and worn by the flow of millions of gallons of blood drawn from the veins of sacrificial goats and bullocks as an atonement for sin. This was their religion. They were sincere. They believed it, lived by it, and died by it!

Or look for a moment at a few of the contemporary pathways men are following in their search for God.

At the break of dawn in a humid hotel room in Cairo, Egypt, I was awakened by a mournful cry outside my window. In the middle of the street was an Arab, kneeling on a rug.

With water from a battered aluminum tea kettle, he carefully washed his hands, his feet, and his face in a ritual of purification. He then prostrated himself toward Mecca and began the first of five prayers that he, and millions of other devout Moslems, would pray that day. This is his religion. He is sincere. He believes it. He lives by it. He is willing to die by it!

Or go with me inside the church of the Holy Sepulcher in Jerusalem. See the marble slab believed by the Catholic world to be the very table on which the crucified body of our Lord was laid out for anointment and prepared for burial. Kneeling beside that slab is a little pilgrim. She has come from afar to this most blessed and sacred place. She makes the sign of the cross. She kisses the slab again and again. She carefully rubs each prayer bead against the sacred stone. Then, with outstretched hands, she scoops up an unseen substance from the slab and rubs and bathes her body with this magical blessedness. Finally, completely covered by this protective and healing blessedness, she arises to go. See in her face the rapture of piety and ecstasy. This is her religion and she is sincere. She believes it. She lives by it! She is willing to die by it!

Or look again. Deep in the African bush a fat, half-naked, ebony woman wrings the head of a scrawny chicken and lets the blood squirt out on a grotesgue and obscene mud idol. The missionary at my side explained. "The mother is giving thanks to her god for a baby." For this is her religion. She is sincere. She lives by it! She is willing to die by it!

The Universality of Religion

This is a panoramic view of the religious activities of men on three continents through seven thousand years of recorded history. As we survey this profusion of religion, religion everywhere, what shall we say? Three great truths are now obvious.

First, there is obviously in the heart of all men an *instinct* for God. This eternal searching and seeking after God is not the result of *external* circumstances, stimulated by fear or crises. It is motivated from *within,* a gnawing hunger for God and a nameless longing for the peace of fellowship with him. Like the instinct that draws a migratory bird to the northern nesting ground, so there is ingrained in the very fiber of the man's soul this instinct that calls him to God. This instinct is universal to all mankind, common to every generation—whether civilized or primitive, contemporary or neolithic, educated or uneducated, cultured or barbarian.

This universal instinct for God is also unique to man alone, of all God's creatures. There are other instincts common to higher forms of life—the instincts for reproduction, self-preservation, and gregarious activity. But only man has an instinct for God, seeks God, and develops systems of worship, prayer, and sacrifice in an effort to find God.

As Christians, we know why this instinct for God is implanted in man. We know that man was made by God, in the image of God, for fellowship with God. But sin defaced that image, drove a wedge, and separated man from God. Thus natural man is alienated from God, at cross purposes with God. Made by God, in the image of God, for fellowship with God, separated and alienated from God by sin—man is universally, uniquely, instinctively, eternally seeking God. Greater in man than any other drive is this nameless, insatiable, instinctive longing for God.

Every man must find something greater than himself and beyond himself to which he gives himself as he seeks to satisfy the frustration of his finiteness, his weakness, his guilt, and his lostness. He has an instinct for God that must be satisfied. Thus, he seeks God in physical form as an idol, or in his business, or in a cause, or in some organized system of religion.

Now, the second truth is this: The expression of this unique and universal instinct for God is what we call "religion." Religion is the instinctive upreach of man for God; the upward thrust of the monoliths of Egypt; the upward reach of the broken pillars of the temple of Jupiter in Athens; the towering alabaster minaret of the Moslem mosque in Damascus calling men to prayer; or the clapboard steeple of a country church on a grassy hillside, pointing like a finger to God. Religion is man instinctively seeking God.

We have been told that what this world now needs is religion. Statesmen and scientists, politicians and philosophers have been calling for a "return to religion." But man has never been without religion. Man could no more live without religion than he could live without air to breathe. Like Paul on Mars' Hill, we find that men turn to a thousand gods every day. The primitive native in the Congo worships a god of mud, while the brilliant university professor worships the white god of science. A Hindu mother in India pours out her sacrifice before a god of bronze, while a young matron down the street makes a god of her family. Even the communist, who says there is no God, makes a god of materialism, a religion of his political philosophy, and he is a zealous missionary for his cause. Today, there is no lack of religion—sincere religion, devout religion, pious religion, fervent religion, personal religion, or organized religion. Religion is everywhere.

Remember our truths. First, all men are instinctively religious. Second, religion is the upreach of man for God. And of religion, there is no lack! Now, a final truth: One religion *is* as good as another. It really makes no difference which path you take because you do not come to know the living God by way of any religion. All the religion in the world cannot reconcile man to God. Futility is the end of all religion.

The Futility of Religion

One religion is as good as another, but Christianity is not a religion. Christianity and religion are opposites.

Religion and Christianity are opposites in *direction*. Religion is the upreach of man for God; Christianity is the downreach of God for man.

Religion and Christianity are opposites in *motivation*. Religion is created out of man's need for God; Christianity stems out of God's grace and love for man.

Religion and Christianity are opposites in *initiation*. Religion is a frustrated man searching for God; Christianity is a compassionate God seeking man.

Religion and Christianity are opposites in *salvation*. Religion is predicated on the belief that man can save himself by acts of worship, rites, ritual, deeds, good works, vicarious service, and devotion. But in Christianity men are saved, not by what they do in penitence and sacrifice, but by what God has already done by his sacrifice of Jesus Christ.

This world is cursed and damned today by a popular idea that religion will save a man. Hell will be filled with sincere religionists who believed that being religious was sufficient. It is not a turning *to* religion, but a turning *from* religion to Christ that will deliver us. Our salvation lies not in what *we do* for God, but in how we respond to what *God has done* already for us on the cross. Our message is not that of the Old Testament prophets of religion calling men to come to God. We are New Testament evangels proclaiming that *God has come to men* through his incarnate son, Jesus Christ.

The Bridge to God

Let me graphically illustrate the distinction between religion and Christianity. Imagine the wall to your right as a great precipice or cliff; the wall to your left as another; and the room between as a bottomless and an impassable chasm of separation. On your side is man; on the other is God. Beginning with Adam in Eden, the erosion of centuries of sin cut deep and wide this great abyss separating man from God.

Here to the left is man. Instinctively he knows that somewhere across this impenetrable vastness on the other side is God, the one who made him, the one whom he belongs. The common necessity, instinctive and universal to all men, is to bridge this gap of sin and get back in fellowship with God.

The bridges men build toward God we call "religion." The bridges, in number and variety, are as multitudinous as the stars of the sky and the sands of the sea. In the Los Angeles telephone directory, under the classified section of religion, you will find listed over 100 strange religions and sects, including 22 Mormon wards, 5 institutes of Religious Science, 2 Scienceology churches, 11 Spiritualist churches, a Lotus Temple, the Agasha Temple of Wisdom, the Center of Illumination, the Ethical Culture Society, the "I Am" Accredited Sanctuary, the Los Angeles Church of World Messianity, and the Self-Realization Church of All Religions.

This is religion, the bridges men build to find God. Some of these bridges are broad and massive, and many are the men who labor to build them. Other bridges are small, with a single builder and only a few travelers.   Some bridges reach out farther toward God than others, since they are more ethical; more acceptable philosophically; or more appealing to the mystical, scientific, or spiritual mind.

All these bridges have two things in common. First, they are built by men of corruptible materials. Second, no bridge ever spans the chasm and reaches God. Every bridge, sooner or later, collapses under its own weight, and those who have traveled it are plunged into futility.

On the other side of this chasm of sin is God. With a broken heart he surveys the frantic and futile efforts of lost men trying to save themselves. By the grace that was in his heart from the foundation of the world, he said, "I will build a bridge over to man and open up for him a way of salvation and restoration." And so the Bible says that "when the fulness of the time was come, God sent forth his Son" (Gal. 4:4). The bridge from God to man! And he was "found in fashion as a man," born of the virgin Mary, at Bethlehem of Judea. At a specific time and in a specific place, God broke through from his side into history. Through Jesus, he came to us because we could not get to him.

For thirty-three years he was "Immanuel," God with us, as he labored in the flesh to establish the bridgehead. Again and again, with infinite patience and care he explained his mission from the Father to man. "I and *my* Father are one."

"The living Father hath sent me." "For God so loved the world, that he gave his only begotten Son." With many miracles, signs, and indisputable proofs of his deity, he drove down the stakes again and again to make secure this end of the bridge. He fed the thousands, healed the blind, made the lame to walk, and cured the demon possessed. Finally, he stood by the tomb of Lazarus and prayed, "Father, . . . that they may believe that thou hast sent me." And he called with a loud voice, "Come forth." And he who had been dead four days came out alive.

When all things had thus been accomplished, Jesus was betrayed and arrested, passed through a night of abuse and torture at the hands of cruel men, and finally was sentenced to die because he "claimed to be God." On that black Friday, they led him through the Damascus gate, out of the city to a rocky limestone outcropping called the Skull.

Stand with me and watch as they stretch his body upon that cross and drive great nails through his hands and feet to make this Calvary. See the squadron of soldiers hoist the heavy cross into the air, tilt it, and let it drop into the hole. See his body sag heavily as his flesh is torn by the scalding nails. For six hours, see him hang there, forsaken by his disciples, jeered by the crowd, tormented by his enemies, and railed at by a thief.

Finally, he lifts his face to the Father and cries, "It is finished." The tormentors scream in delight, "Hear him. He is delirious. *He* is finished. We shall never again hear of the carpenter of Nazareth." But he cries again, "No! No! *It* is finished." And he dies.

They were wrong. He was not finished. Three days later, He came up from the grave, alive forevermore. As the living Lord he has marched through the centuries gathering millions in his train. Every tick of the clock moves us closer to that victory when the kingdoms of this world shall become the kingdom of our Lord. *He* was not finished; *it* was finished.

What was finished? The bridge! God's way of salvation! The bridge of reconciliation, built first in the heart of God from the foundation of the world and finished at crimson Calvary. Standing beside that bridge Jesus says, "I am the way, the truth, and the life: no man cometh unto the Father, but by me." There is no other way to God, to reconciliation, and fellowship with him save by Jesus Christ.

You do not come to the living God over the bridge of any religion. You do not come to God by the bridge of religious rites and acts of worship. You do not come to God by way of the bridge of the church. You do not come to God by way of the bridge of baptism. You do not come to God over a bridge built out of your good works and clean conduct. There is only one way, God's way, the way of Jesus Christ.

And the good news that is ours to proclaim is that every man stands within two steps of this bridge with the promise of Jesus that "him that cometh unto me I will in no wise cast out." The first step onto this bridge is *repentance*. To repent means to turn from every other way, every other hope, every other bridge, every sin, and turn to Jesus as the only way.

The second step is to *believe*. Believe *on* the bridge. I may believe it is a bridge, and know all the facts about when and where it was built, and how it was built, and by whom it was built. But this knowledge and belief about the bridge never gets me to the other side. When I believe *on* the bridge, exercise my will as a free moral agent, and start walking in trust across that bridge, putting the safety and destiny of my life on it—only then does the bridge bear me up to the other side. The glorious good news of the gospel is that any man can come to Jesus. By these two simple steps, he can pass over from death to life and be eternally reconciled to God!

Notes

Chapter 1

1. *Wall Street Journal* (New York), January 29, 1958, p. 13.
2. *Sermons of the Week,* II (August 10, 1960), 21.
3. *Commercial Appeal* (Memphis), May 13, 1961, p. 6.
4. *Press-Scimitar* (Memphis), May 4, 1961, p. 7.
5. J. Edgar Hoover, "Communist Propaganda and the Christian Pulpit," *Christianity Today,* V (October 24, 1960), 6.
6. Ralph Lord Roy, *Communism and the Churches* (New York: Harcourt, Brace and Co., 1960).
7. *Jackson Sun,* June 21, 1959, p. 9.
8. *Press-Scimitar* (Memphis), May 3, 1961, p. 4.
9. Josef Rysan, "Communism, a Secular Religion in the Making," *Vanderbilt Alumnus,* May—June, 1961, p. 14 ff.
10. J. Edgar Hoover, "Soviet Rule or Christian Renewal?" *Christianity Today,* V (November 7, 1960), 10 f. Used by permission.
11. *Ibid.,* p. 8.

Chapter 2

1. Hoover, "Communist Propaganda and the Christian Pulpit," *op. cit.,* p. 5.
2. Hoover, "Soviet Rule or Christian Renewal?" *op. cit.,* p. 8.

Chapter 3

1. P. A. Sorokin, "The Depth of the Sex Crisis," *Christianity Today,*

IV (July 4, 1960), 3 ff. Used by permission.

2. Howard Whitman, "Divorce Granted," *Reader's Digest,* LXV (October, 1954), 11-16.

Chapter 4

1. Jack Finegan, *Space, Atoms and God* (St. Louis: Bethany Press, 1959), p. 33.
2. *Ibid.,* p. 34.
3. *Ibid.,* p. 35.
4. John McPartland, "No Go, Space Cadet," *Harper's Magazine,* CCIV (May, 1952), 66.
5. Ben Hecht, *Esquire* (November, 1958), p. 67. Copyright 1958 by Esquire, Inc.
6. Warren Weaver, "Can a Scientist Believe in God?" *Look,* XIX (April 5, 1955), 27-31. Used by permission.
7. Wernher von Braun, "Seven Mysteries of Space," *This Week Magazine* (September 13, 1959), p. 18.
8. Weaver, *op. cit.*
9. John B. Medaris, "A General Looks at God," *This Week Magazine* (September 13, 1959), p. 2.
10. *This Week Magazine* (January 24, 1960), p. 2. Reprinted from THIS WEEK Magazine. Copyright 1960 by the United Newspapers Magazine Corporation.
11. Robert E. D. Clark, "The Heart of the Problem," *Christianity Today,* III (May 11, 1959), 3-5. Used by permission.
12. Copyright 1948 by Percy B. Crawford. Used by permission.

Chapter 5

1. *Commercial Appeal* (Memphis), April 3, 1960, p. 14.
2. *Ibid.*
3. Millard J. Berquist, *Southern Baptist Preaching* (Nashville: Broadman Press, 1959), p. 46.
4. *Commercial Appeal* (Memphis), April 3, 1960, p. 14.
5. Berquist, *op. cit.,* p. 47.
6. *Ibid.*
7. Horace E. Campbell, "Drinking Drivers Are Getting Away with Murder," *Family Weekly* (March 13, 1960), p. 1.
8. Berquist, *op. cit.,* p. 48.
9. *Ibid.*

Chapter 6

1. Eduardo Krapf, "Who Are They?" *World Health,* State Department Bulletin, May—June, 1960, p. 30.
2. George Kent, "Once More—VD," *Reader's Digest,* LXXVIII (March, 1961), 86 ff.
3. Clark W. Blackburn, "New American Tragedy: School Girl Mothers," *This Week Magazine* (June 8, 1958), p. 14.
4. This information is derived from Sheldon and Eleanor Glueck, *Unraveling Juvenile Delinquency,* Cambridge, Massachusetts, Harvard University Press, for the Commonwealth Fund, 1950.
5. Jack Harrison Pollock, "What Makes Families Happy?" *This Week Magazine* (September 13, 1959), p. 11.

Chapter 7

1. *Survey Bulletin,* Vol. XVI (Nashville: Sunday School Board of the Southern Baptist Convention, May 26, 1961).
2. Leo Rosten (ed.), *Guide to the Religions of America* (New York: Simon & Schuster, Inc., 1955).
3. *Sunday Visitor,* XLIX (April 16, 1961), 2.
4. W. Stanford Reid, "Protestant-Roman Union: 25 Scholars' Views," *Christianity Today,* V (October 10, 1960), 32.
5. *Sunday Visitor, op. cit.*
6. *Baptist and Reflector,* January 12, 1961, p. 5.
7. "Minority Report, Southern Baptist Convention, Baltimore, Maryland, June 14, 1940," *Quarterly Review,* April, 1951, p. 56.

Chapter 8

1. *Baptist Beacon,* January 19, 1961, p. 5.
2. *Ibid.*
3. *Ibid.*
4. *Everson* v. *Board of Education,* 330 U. S. 1 (1947).
5. *Christian Science Monitor* (Boston), February 1, 1954, p. 3.
6. C. Stanley Lowell, "Rising Tempo of Rome's Demands," *Christianity Today,* I (January 7, 1957), 13.
7. *Baptist Standard,* February 22, 1961, p. 16.
8. Lowell, *op. cit.*
9. *Rocky Mountain Baptist,* April 21, 1961, p. 5.
10. C. Stanley Lowell, "Mandate and Mission: What Is the Church's

Real Task?" *Christianity Today,* V (March 13, 1961), 28.
11. *Report from the Capitol,* July 13, 1961, p. 4.
12. *Baptist Standard,* April 19, 1961, p. 5.
13. John A. Ryan and Francis J. Boland, *Catholic Principles of Politics* (New York: The Macmillan Co., 1940), pp. 320-21.
14. *Ibid.,* p. 318.
15. *Raleigh Times,* February 10, 1961, p. 12.